Becoming God's Friend

Let Every Day Be an Adventure with God

Barbara G. Miller

Becoming God's Friend:
Let Every Day Be an Adventure with God

Copyright 2016 by Barbara G. Miller

ISBN-13: 978-1535364362

ISBN-10: 153536436X

Cover Image photographed by Joe Gallegos, son-in-law of author, Sunset in Costa Rica

Edited by MariLee Parrish

Printed in the United States of America

Most Scripture quotations are from:
The New King James version of the Bible

God's or the Holy Spirit's words to me are shown in italics.

Foreword by *Lindsey Waymire:

When I first met Barbara last spring (2009) at a Storytellers training session, I have to confess that I quickly jumped to the wrong conclusion about her. The women sitting around the table that afternoon were pretty boisterous; pretty clear and outspoken about their stories. Barbara was soft-spoken. She held the details of her story close to her. She quoted scripture to comfort one woman who was upset. And she even sang a few lines from a scripture song during her talk. "What a sweet church lady" I quickly decided. Someone who knows God, Scripture and hymns, but kept this as a separate quadrant to life. A bit of a Polly-Anna. Having no idea what her story or her life was full of.

My stereotype of her was blown away as she shared her story. By the end of that session I was trying to figure out how I could spend more time with Barbara so I could learn more about her simple trust in the Lord. The simple way she talked to her heavenly Father and the powerful comfort and deep satisfaction that comes from her personal intimate relationship.

The kind I long for.

Barbara and Lori Wurth attended "The Stories" Ministry at First Presbyterian Church in Boulder which was led by Lindsay Waymire. This was the first time Barbara shared her story publicly of losing Richard and how God prepared her and got her through it.

From the Editor:

Scripture Songs

Let the message of Christ dwell among you richly as you teach and admonish one another with all wisdom through psalms, hymns, and songs from the Spirit, singing to God with gratitude in your hearts. Colossians 3:16

If there was just one scripture in all of God's Word that completely captured Barbara Miller's life as I knew her, it is this one! If anyone spent any amount of time with her, Barbara would most definitely break into scripture songs at some point in the conversation.

The first time I heard her do this, I was amazed at the complete freedom this woman had in Christ! She knew she was God's child and that He loved to hear from her. Many of her friends will tell you that they were a bit startled the first time they were in a conversation with Barbara and heard her break into song. She did so with no fanfare, just like it was a normal part of every discussion. Her songs were encouraging and completely fitting with whatever issue was at hand.

We all came to love and expect this from Barbara over time. She was literally fulfilling this scripture singing "songs from the Spirit"…with gratitude in her heart!

Introduction and Acknowledgments

My Story

I want people to know that they can be friends with the God of the universe. I'm just an ordinary woman who felt God's hand drawing me to become His friend while I was very young.

As I grew in the Lord I began learning more about God's grace and how important the Holy Spirit was to our growing and changing to be more like Jesus. My life has been a life of learning to be dependent on the Holy Spirit and learning to love the Lord with all my heart, all my soul, all my mind, and to love my neighbor as myself.

Love is the key to our walk and living God's word is what brings change into our life.

Why I Wrote This Book

For many years I struggled with the thoughts of writing a book about how God worked in my life. When I was with a friend I found myself telling her a story about an event that seemed to relate to her life. She would then say to me, "You should write a book of the stories that you tell. They are so helpful."

This happened so often that I began to think about this as something God wanted me to do. I even took a correspondence writing class for children's stories. This led to a marionette puppet ministry and writing stories for my marionette puppets to perform to. After several years of doing the marionette puppet shows, I still did not begin to work on writing a book about my life stories.

Many years passed and I was asked to be a Mother's of Pre-Schoolers (MOPS) mentor, this gave me the opportunity to share my life stories with these young mothers. These young ladies encouraged me to write my stories in a book so they could be remembered. They came up with a plan: They signed up for a day to visit me. I would tell a story and they would type it on the computer. I want to thank each one of these girls who believed in me, who stood by me and supported me: Lori Wurth, Samantha Gibbs, Christy Glaze, Nicole Wilson, Caitlyn Lechuga and Jenni Lovins.

I also want to thank my daughter for her patience. Without her, this book would not have been accomplished. I want to give a special Thank You to MariLee for helping with the editing and getting my book published. Thanks to all who made this dream come true.

I believe Our Loving Lord has long wanted me to complete this task. Even when I procrastinated for so many years, He never gave up on me. Praise God for His loving kindness. I need his help every moment.

My Calling from God

I started in 1981 writing in a journal and having a quiet time. This was the beginning of the most exciting adventure I have ever encountered. God always has time for me and He makes me feel like I am His favorite daughter.

One of the disciplines I began was to read the Bible each morning. As I read the Word I began seeing that my ways were far from God's ways. I asked God to renew my mind. I needed a lot of help. God had promised to give us His Holy Spirit and sometime later the Holy Spirit spoke to my heart. He showed me His plan for my life:

Your Heavenly Father loves you and created you to live a life pleasing to him and to know him intimately.

I have fashioned you for a vessel of prayer. Many can speak for Me and many carry My word, but few pursue the path of prayer. Never doubt your worth, never turn from this path. Know that you are needed and that My hand has molded you for this very purpose.

Table of Contents

Chapter 1

Early Life

I believe the loving relationship I had with my earthly father during my early life helped me to know and love my heavenly Father. Each story shows how I was taught by the Holy Spirit.

Daddy's Helper

Isaiah 38:19
The living, the living man, he shall praise you, as I
do this day; the father shall make known Your truth
to the children.

When I was a little girl my mother went to
work and I was left at home with my Daddy, who
was a farmer. He would take me on the tractor with
him and I would sit on his lap and he treated me
very special. We fed the cows and pigs together. I
was his little sidekick. He gave me jobs to do when
he did his chores. I felt important and I enjoyed
working with my Daddy. I knew he loved having
me as his little helper. We had fun together.

Because I had this loving relationship with
my Daddy, I believe it helped me know my
Heavenly Father more intimately when I grew up
and began learning about God. Many people who
have had bad relationships with their earthly fathers
have difficulty trusting God as a loving Father.

My Daddy Taught Me
the Meaning of Forgiveness

Ephesians 4:32
Be kind to one another, tender-hearted, forgiving
one another, even as God in Christ forgave you.

I had a friend, Judy, who lived on the farm
next to us. One day she came to play. We decided
to put some of my toys in the wagon and take them
back to the pig house in the woods. Then we
decided we needed a stove to bake our mud pies on.
So, we took two bricks and a piece of wood across
the top and set our little pies on our homemade
stove.

Then, Judy suggested we get some matches
and start a fire in our stove. I told her I didn't think
that would be a good idea.

"They will never get baked this way," she
said. So we went up to the house and got some
matches, we ran quickly back to our pig house and
gathered some twigs to start our fire.

While the pies were baking, we decided to
go "hunting." When we looked back at the pig
house we saw smoke. We ran over to see what was
happening. To our surprise the pig house was on
fire!

My father and Judy's father had seen the
smoke and came to put out the fire. I remember
running to my Daddy and I hugged his leg and told

him I was very sorry. I said, "Daddy, I'm so sorry I'll never do that again."

Judy and her father left. Daddy said to me, "I don't believe you will ever do anything like this again. I really believe the scare was enough punishment so I'm not going to spank you."

I laid on my Daddy's chest and cried tears of thanksgiving. I knew I had the very best father anyone could have.

The next day, Judy came to see me. "What did your Dad do to you?" she asked.

"Nothing," I said. "He knew I was truly sorry and I wouldn't do anything like that again. What did your Dad do?"

She pulled up her shirt and showed me the welts on her back. She said, "I wish your Daddy was my daddy."

I realized how loved I was.

Don't Do That

Proverbs 16:9
A man's heart plans his way, but the Lord directs his steps.

At one point when I was little, my mother left my father and went to stay with her brother. I don't remember if she said why or even how long she was gone. I just remember how sad we were. She must have been gone for some time because my Dad's mother came to stay with our family.

One day, I asked my grandmother, "Where is my Daddy?"

"He is probably out in the barn someplace," she said. So, I went to look for him.

I noticed the corncrib door at the end of the barn was ajar. I pulled it open and there was my Daddy, sitting up on the top rung of the corncrib with a rope around his neck. I screamed at him, "Daddy get down! Don't do that!"

I ran to get my grandma and I told her that my daddy needed help. We ran to the barn and when she saw what my daddy was doing, she told me to go back to the house.

I remember Grandma called my mother and we children all got on the phone and cried and begged her to come home, because we were very sad.

She came back home and never left again. But she was a very unhappy person. I'm sure I was very confused and would have benefited if someone had taken the time to talk to me about what was happening. As a child I was never taught to pray or even that there was a God. Even though no one told me about God I have no doubt to this day that God had His hand on me.

God Used Me to Lead the Way

Philippians 1:6
Being confident of this very thing, that He who has
began a good work in you will complete it until the
day of Jesus Christ.

When my father was young he went to the
Pentecostal church with his parents. As an adult, he
decided he was never going back to church again.
Consequently, I didn't go to church. But God
started drawing me and placing a desire to know
Him in my heart. When I was a freshman in High
School I decided I would walk to the church that
was down the road from our house. It was
Ebenezer Lutheran Church.

It was there that I took catechism, was
baptized, and became a member of this church.
When I was baptized I invited my parents to come
to church to witness the event. After that they began
going to church with me. I believe this is how God
used me to lead my family back to Him.

God's Protection

II Timothy 4:18
The Lord will deliver me from every evil work and
preserve me for His heavenly kingdom. To Him be
the glory forever and ever. Amen

As I look back over my life, I realize that
God protected me from misconceptions about God
and Jesus and the Holy Spirit, that so many people
are burdened with because of false teachings. I'm
glad that the church that God first lead me to gave
me a sure foundation. I was taught that God's word
is true and acceptable.

I hope that this book will help others to
except the gifts that God gives to us through the
Holy Spirit. He is a person. He has feelings, and
can be accepted as your true helper. I don't
understand how a person cannot accept the truth
that our bodies are the temple of the Holy Spirit.
This gives us the power to live a grace filled life. It
is a gift from our Heavenly Father. Our prayer life
is dependent on His gift to us. This protection has
helped me have a better relationship with my Father
in Heaven.

These stories have helped me become the
person I am today. I believe my stories can help the
reader see how important prayer is in our life. You
may begin to realize that prayer doesn't just change
the person you pray for, but it begins to change you
because of your yielding to the Holy Spirit.

All Things Work Together for Good

Proverbs 19:11
The discretion of a man makes him slow to anger.
And his glory is to overlook a transgression.

As a young woman, I wanted to go to Wittenberg College to become a Deaconess. I filled out all the paperwork and sent it off and now I waited for my acceptance letter, which never came.

Not until on my mother's deathbed did I find out why I was not accepted at Wittenberg.

I said to her one day as I sat by her bed, "Mom, do you know why I never got my Wittenberg acceptance letter?"

"Oh, I am so sorry," she replied. "I threw it away."

I asked her why she had done that. She said, "I was afraid God would take you away from me and call you to be a missionary." I wasn't mad at her; I just couldn't quite understand it.

My story wouldn't be what it is if I had gone to Wittenberg College and become a Deaconess. Even though it looked like my mother thwarted God's plan for me, He used everything that happened for my good and His glory.

Chapter 2

Choosing a Mate

God goes before us and helps us make choices in every area of our life. Choosing a mate is a very important part of a young woman's life. I wanted God's will and I believe He was very involved in helping me choose the right mate.

God's Word Helps Me

Psalm 34:17
The righteous cry out, and the Lord hears, and
delivers them out of all their troubles.

At 17, I found the young man I felt I was
going to marry. He went to a different school than I
did, but his sister Peggy and I had attended the same
junior high school.

One weekend, Peggy invited me to come
and spend the weekend with them. I don't know if I
realized her parents were going to be out of town or
not, but the plan was made.

Donald and I were on the couch watching
TV together. To our surprise, Donald's parents
came home unexpectedly and when they saw us,
they had a few choice words for me. They called
me names I had never heard before and they said,
"In the morning, you will be taken home never to
come back again."

I asked for a Bible and I spent the rest of the
night on the couch, reading the Psalms, and God's
word helped me have peace.

The next day, as Donald and I drove to my
house, we decided that we were going to run off and
get married. When we drove up to my house, to my
surprise, my mother's car was in the driveway. I
thought she would be at work.

11

I told Donald to stay in the car and I ran into the house to pack a few clothes. My mother came into my room and asked, "What are you doing?"

I told her, "Donald and I have decided to run off and get married."

She was not surprised, but she had a few words of wisdom to share with me, like: "How are you going to pay for a place to live? Neither one of you have a job. You are not staying here."

I realized that we were acting very foolish and I went out to the car and told Donald, "Listen, we can't do this. You don't have a job. We don't have a place to stay. It just won't work."

And he agreed with me. That was the last time I saw him. His parents moved the family to another town to keep us separated.

My Move to California

I Peter 5:7
Casting all your care on Him, for He cares for you.

During my teenage life it was easy to look back over the incidents and see God's hand leading me to follow His will.

One particular event was going to California for my brother's wedding. It was at the wedding that I met Ramsey, an Arabian, he was my brother's best man and he liked me.

When I went back home he began writing love letters to me and sent me flowers every week. I was overwhelmed by the attention.

When my brother suggested that I come to California and live with him and his wife I was excited, because I would be near Ramsey. When I was able to talk to Ramsey in person I became aware that after he graduated he planned to go back to Arabia and work with his father in their business.

This move didn't appeal to me and I began politely telling Ramsey this move wasn't something that I would consider.

My original plan was to live in California to establish my residency so it would be less expensive to attend college. God had brought me to San Diego, California from Indianapolis, Indiana to meet the man I would eventually marry. Not Ramsey, but a native Californian.

Across the street from my brother's house was a girl who was friends with a young man named Richard. He had recently been discharged from the Army. She invited me to go to the beach with her. Richard would be coming, too. This was the beginning of a lasting friendship between Richard and I. We went to the beach every day and we had a lot of fun together.

Who will it be, Carl or Richard?

Proverbs 5:21
For the ways of man are before the eyes of the Lord,
and He ponders all his paths.

At school I met a young man named Carl. He was a perfect gentleman and treated me like a queen. We went on dates and I was becoming very accustomed to being treated like a queen. I had come to realize that God seems to give you choices in your life. I had already made a choice to break my relationship with Ramsey and now I had another choice: Carl or Richard. Did I want to be treated like a queen or live a life of fun and laughter?

When Carl asked me to marry him I thought God had opened the door for me to live as a queen with love and special treatment. I was thrilled! We bought a ring and Carl took me to meet his parents. I thought my life was going to be complete.

When I came home and showed my brother my ring he was surprised and he asked me "Where does Richard fit in?"

I told him that Richard was only a good friend. My brother just laughed. The next day I went with Richard to the beach. We had lunch, laughed and talked, but not about Carl.

When I got home, my sister-in-law asked, "How did Richard take the news?"

"I didn't tell him," I said. "The thought of not seeing Richard ever again is breaking my heart. I guess I love Richard and not Carl."

I realized that getting treated like a queen would lose its charm but a friendship would continue to grow strong.

When Carl came that evening I said "Carl I want to give you back this ring, I realize that I am too young to commit to a marriage."

Carl took me in his arms and cried. He said "I will wait for you!"

I said "I'm not what you think I am, forgive me, I just can't meet up to your expectations. Eventually I would be destroyed trying."

We stopped seeing each other. I realized that God had given me the wisdom to make this decision.

Richard had never talked about marriage, but I knew I had a friend... and if God wanted me to marry him, He would have to work it out. God knows best. I trusted Him for directing my life. He had helped me with David, Ramsey, Carl, and I believed that He was going to work out my life with Richard.

Getting to Know Richard

I Corinthians 13:4-6
Love suffers long and is kind; love does not envy;
love does not parade itself, is not puffed up; does
not behave rudely, does not seek its own, is not
provoked, thinks no evil; does not rejoice in
iniquity, but rejoices in the truth;

After I broke up with Carl, I started going on dates with Richard. On our first date he took me to a fancy restaurant. When I said, "This is a beautiful place. I'm impressed." He said, "Jane liked it last weekend, so I thought you would like it too."

A few weeks later we went to a party and I asked him to come and open the car door for me. He asked, "You got a broken arm?" He got out and left me sitting in the car.

After a half an hour, I decided to swallow my pride and go inside. I never asked him to open my door again. I realized I was trying to make him more like Carl, because I really liked being treated like a special lady.

What was I going to do? Had I made the wrong choice? I decided to stick with Richard and see what God had planned for us.

Chapter 3

My Husband

Like all marriages, we change with time.
Richard's personality had been shaped by his
family, his time in the Army, and his friends.
Maybe it was the responsibility of supporting
and raising a family, but the fun-loving young
man that I married changed over time...
as we all do.

Our Marriage

Genesis 2:18
And the Lord God said, "It is not good that man
should be alone; I will make him a helper
comparable to him."

Richard asked me to marry him in July of
1958. Our wedding was at the Pacific Beach
Lutheran Church. We spent our honeymoon in the
mountains. It was perfect weather and we kept the
convertible top down as we drove. We enjoyed tent
camping and hiking, and cooking our meals over
the campfire. We enjoyed talking and laughing
together. It was a great start to our marriage. And I
knew the scripture that told me that I was to be my
husband's helper. How God was going to bring this
to pass was a mystery.

Before our wedding we had bought a trailer
and moved it to a trailer park on the bay. After our
honeymoon we moved into our new trailer together.
We made new friends with our neighbors and
enjoyed swimming and water skiing with them after
work.

In February of 1959 our first daughter was
born. We now had to change our life style… there
would be less beach parties, and more time spent
with grandparents. After two years we had a second
daughter. We had out-grown our trailer at that point
so we began looking for a house. We found an
older couple who were retiring and wanted to buy a

trailer. This was perfect for us, so we bought their house and they bought our trailer.

Surprise, Surprise

John 19:34
One of the soldiers pierced His side with a spear
and immediately blood and water came out.

After we were married for a few months we started going to a Sunday school class at the Lutheran church. This included discussions about the Bible. My first surprise was that Richard's beliefs weren't the same as mine. He had misconceptions that Jesus truly died for our sins and was raised from the dead. I wanted to convince him of the truth, but God would have to be the one who would teach him... not me.

I asked him one time, "what do you believe?"

"Well the Bible is just a bunch of stories, whoever wrote it had a good imagination!" He said.

"What do you mean?" I asked.

"The story about Moses parting the Red Sea" he answered.

I told him that I believed it was a miracle. How else would you explain it? And he said "A few miles up the sea some land started falling into the water and caused a dam to prevent the water from rushing down. So then they could walk across without any harm."

I said "Well I guess the miracle was that it happened exactly when Moses was ready to cross it."

"Believe what you want…" he said.

"How about Jesus dying on the cross and being raised again?" I asked.

"Jesus had been through a lot, they took Him off the cross, they put Him in this nice cool tomb, He was revived, pushed the stone away and left," he said.

I said nothing. I just offered it up to God and said, "This man needs Your help."

I tried to not say any more about what he believed or what I believed. Rather than trying to teach Richard the truth, I decided to pray for him to have the Holy Spirit reveal the truth to him.

The event that God used to show Richard the truth was several years later. We went to my mom and dad's house and my mother said, "Let's go to the art museum" so we all got in the car and went to the museum. We entered one room that had a painting of the crucifixion. Richard stood in front of that painting and saw Jesus on the cross and the Roman guard, thrusting that sword into Jesus' side. It was so vivid because it was life size.

His comment was "I'll be damned. He really did die!"

Now my prayer was, "Father, you will have to show Richard that Jesus was truly raised from the dead."

I Made a Plan

Proverbs 3:5-6
Trust in the Lord with all your heart, and lean not
on your own understanding; in all your ways
acknowledge Him and He shall direct your paths.

Just as most young couples have problems, Richard and I were not unique. Every Friday night was Richard's night to go out with the guys. My parents had come to visit us and I asked Richard, "Please, don't go out with the guys, just come home."

"They're having a party and I'm going to the party," he said.

After he left, I called the office and found out where the party was. I began to have a plan. I asked my father to take me to the person's house, where the party was and leave me there. He said, "I don't think this is a good idea."

"Yes," I said. "It's something that has to be done, Dad."

I got out of the car, walked up to the upstairs apartment where the party was and stood there ready to knock on the door, but I couldn't. I turned around, walked down the stairs and knocked on the door of the apartment below where the party was. When they answered the door I asked, "Can I use your phone?" They agreed and let me come in to use the phone. I was so glad that I had brought the phone number with me for the person who was having the party.

I called the apartment upstairs and asked to speak to Richard. When he came to the phone I said, "Richard, would you please come and take me home?"

"Where are you?" He asked.

"I'm at the apartment underneath where you are," I answered.

"I'll be there shortly," he said.

We got into the car and left. He said to me, "When you get home, I want you to pack your clothes and the kids' clothes and ask your mom and dad to take you with them back to Indiana."

I made no comment. But I cried to the Lord "I need Your help."

When we got home, Richard said, "Get out!" I got out and he sped away in anger.

When I got inside, my father said, "Where's Richard?"

I told him, "He's gone back to the party. He was a little angry."

My father said, "I didn't think it was a good idea."

I answered, "Yes it was, Dad. Goodnight, I'm going to bed."

Richard came home, got in bed, said nothing about what had happened and we never spoke of it again. But he never went to another Friday night party again. Praise God.

Lord Change Me!

Luke 15:7
I say to you likewise there will be more joy in
heaven over one sinner who repents, than over
ninety-nine just persons, who need no repentance.

After being married for several years, I fell out of love with my husband because he had changed. He was no longer friendly and fun to be with. He was now controlling and called me stupid a lot. I decided that the best way to deal with it was to leave. I didn't tell anybody that I was leaving, but just left my kids, my home, and my life as it was.

As I was driving down the road to meet a man of my choosing, who was a "Christian", the Holy Spirit asked me, *"What are you doing?"*

"I am going to run off with Bob, who is a 'Christian' and who loves me," I replied.

As I drove to meet him, the Holy Spirit helped me think, *"What are you going to do when this man gets tired of you just like he has with his wife now?"*

That had never occurred to me. So I began thinking about this as a possibility. I turned the car around and went to the church and knelt down at the altar and told God, "I've made a mess of my life, and I don't know if it can be repaired. But I'm willing if You will create love in my heart for Richard."

I had the assurance in my spirit that God would help me. So I went back home that very day.

When I got there, it was a new beginning. That night when I went to bed, Richard reached out and touched my shoulder. At the time, my way of dealing with his touch was to turn my back to him. But this time I was reminded that I had asked for love to be created in my heart for this man. That was something I did not believe could happen... but with faith I began walking in the ways that God pointed me to walk.

The first change that He wanted to be brought about was for me to walk in the Scripture, *to submit unto my husband as unto the Lord.* I began to walk in submission as God showed me how. It became the most beautiful experience that I have ever encountered.

God began showing me how to do things that were acts of love towards my husband. He gave me things to say that would show respect to my husband rather than putting him down.

God held up His part of the bargain by creating love in my heart for Richard again. And to the day he died we had a loving relationship that I could never have created on my own.

God Gives His Help

Genesis 2:20
*So Adam gave names to all cattle, to the birds of the
air, and to every beast of the field. But for Adam
there was not found a helper comparable to him.*

In my devotions I began reading scripture
with a new perspective. It was for me to live, not
just read.

The first scripture that God brought into my
mind was Ephesians 5:22 *"Submit unto your
husband as unto the Lord."* I cried, "Could we have
a different one?

"No" was the answer.

Again, I said, "I need Your help, I don't
want to become a doormat."

And God said, *"If you do it my way, you
won't become a doormat. You will become a
helpmate for your husband."*

I asked God "Please create in my heart love
for this man." And he agreed.

God began showing me things to do that
created love between us. Richard noticed a
difference in me and said, "What's happened to
you?"

"Well, God told me to follow the scripture, submit to your husband as unto the Lord, and I'm trying to do that."

"How long has that been in the Bible?" Richard asked.

"Forever, but I didn't want to walk in obedience to it." I said. "There's one for you to walk in too. If you'd like, I'll tell you."

"Can't promise you anything, but what is it?" Richard asked.

I quoted the scripture, "Love your wives like Christ loved the church and died for her."

Richard's response was, "He doesn't make it easy does He?"

Leading of the Holy Spirit

Romans 12:2
And do not be conformed to this world, but be
transformed by the renewing of your mind, that you
may prove what is that good and acceptable and
perfect will of God.

Once when Richard was sitting in his chair,
the Holy Spirit told me: "*Run your fingers through
his hair.*" And when I did this, Richard would reach
up and squeeze my hand.

One night, he was lying on the couch
watching a football game and the Holy Spirit said,
"*Go lay down and snuggle with him*". I did this.

Then Richard asked me, "What are you
doing here?" so I explained that the Holy Spirit had
told me to come and lay down with him.

"Does He like football?" Richard asked.

"I guess so, but I don't," I said.

So we laid and watched football together.
Richard began teaching me a little about football.
This began a fun experience of going to the high
school football games. It was interesting how the
Holy Spirit created things in our life to make us
understand each other so much better.

One thing that the Holy Spirit asked me to do was to read Richard's *Mother Earth* magazine so I could have something to talk about that interested him. He was amazed that I had been reading his magazine. It amazes me how the Holy Spirit will lead us in everything, even small details to help us with our relationships.

Let's Make a Deal

Psalm 95:8-9
Do not harden your hearts, as in the rebellion. As in the day of trial in the wilderness, when your fathers tested Me; they tried Me, though they saw My work.

One day Richard and I were walking down the lane and I said, "Oh God, thank you for making our farm so beautiful!"

"What do you mean God made this so beautiful? I'm the one that did all the work! What did He do?" Richard said.

"Oh Richard, I can't explain to you why I think God has done the work here," I said.

"Ok, I'll make you a deal." He said. "You don't pray and ask for God's help and I will show you that I'm the one who does the work around here!"

"That's a dangerous request, but I agree," I said.

So for the next month or so, I didn't really *not* pray, I just asked God to show Richard that it is God who makes everything.

Guess what?

It rained on the farm across the road from us, but no rain fell on our crops! Other things happened as you might expect, including the cows getting into the corn field and trampling the corn; and the garden didn't do well because of the lack of rain.

One day Richard said to me, "You've proved your point, go ahead and start praying again."

Praise God! We were back on the right path.

Where is the Pipe?

John 15:7
*If you abide in Me and My words abide in you, you
will ask what you desire, and it shall be done for
you.*

Richard had laid a water pipe from the well
down by the road up to our house, which was about
two football fields apart. He had never marked off
where the pipe was buried. And the grass grew up,
so we couldn't tell where it was buried.

Now his plan was to use the water from the
other well to water our garden and animals. So he
began work on this project. The first thing he had to
do was find the pipe. He was working on this when
I came home from church one Sunday. He yelled at
me when I got out of the car.

"Barbara, get over here!"

"What's the matter Richard?" I asked.

"Where is the pipe?" Richard asked.

"You're asking me where the pipe is? I
don't know where the pipe is!"

"Well, do something!" He said.

"Do something? You want me to pray and
ask God where the pipe is? Ok, God, Richard wants
to know where the pipe is?"

The thought that came into my mind was *"Where the shovel hits the dirt, there the pipe will be."* In my mind I said, "I don't think he's going to like that answer."

But I told Richard anyway: "Richard, where the shovel hits the dirt, there the pipe will be."

In anger, he jammed the shovel down into the earth and we heard a "clink".

There the pipe was.

There was no "thank you" from Richard. But I thanked the Lord. I was amazed at God's sense of humor.

Whose Idea?

Psalm 37:23
The steps of a good man are ordered by the Lord,
and He delights in his way.

God came to my aid again. Richard never liked my ideas. I would share an idea with him and he would reject it, but after a few weeks he would come up with an idea. And it would be the same idea I had given him. This made me mad, and so I told God, "I want to be able to know that it was my idea and be acknowledged that it was my idea."

God spoke to me and said, *"Can you accept My idea as being good?"* I agreed that I could.

So I would pray and say, "Okay God, I have this neat idea. If You think it would work and You like it, then you give it to Richard. I won't say anything and I'll know that it was my idea but that You gave it to Richard."

It was easier to receive *"no, that's not a good idea"* from God than it was from my husband.

This worked nicely and it was exciting to know that my husband was hearing from the Holy Spirit. I never made any comment that his idea was from God and I never took credit for it. When this happened I was sure God's idea was good and that God was all knowing, so it helped me trust the

37

outcome. This plan gave me the opportunity to show respect for my husband and it came to pass with love and not as a nagging wife.

Richard's Wisdom

Hebrews 5:1-2
For every high priest taken from among men is appointed for men in things pertaining to God, that he may offer both gifts and sacrifices for sins. He can have compassion on those who are ignorant and going astray, since he himself is also subject to weakness.

I always had an idea that pastors were someone very special and had a better relationship with God than we did. In my conversations with Richard, I would talk about pastors and esteem them.

"You should not do that," Richard said. "Pastors are no different than you or I. You should not put them on a pedestal." I agreed with him and began to look at pastors with new eyes and saw the wisdom in Richard's comment. It was true: I should not put anyone on a pedestal. We are told in scripture that pastors are to equip us and bring the truth to us, so we can be taught God's will. God uses many ways to teach us and pastors have been chosen as God's teachers.

Pastors need prayed for and they are there to help us. But many of us believe that our pastors must come between us and God or that only they know the right thing for us to do. But the truth is that the Holy Spirit is our counselor and we can go directly to Him for answers.

Did He Believe?

Romans 8:34
Who is he who condemns? It is Christ who died,
and further more is also risen, who is even at the
right hand of God, who also makes intercession for
us.

I wanted to know if Richard believed in Jesus and in God so I asked for God to make it clear. One night, shortly after I had prayed this prayer, there was a program on the educational channel about Christianity. I sat there amazed that God had made it so easy for me to bring up this subject.

When the program was over, I asked Richard, "Do you believe in God?"

"Of course, He created heaven and earth." Richard said.

"Do you believe in Jesus?" I asked.

"Yes, I believe in Jesus. He died for us." Richard said.

My heart was pounding with excitement. I prayed a prayer of praise quietly. I had received the answer to my prayer and that satisfied me.

Boring Sermons

Psalm 32:8
I will instruct you and teach you in the way you
should go. I will guide you with My eye.

Kwajalein Island is in the South Pacific between Hawaii and Guam, where the US Army has a military base. This island was only three miles long and a half-mile wide. Richard needed a job when Computer Science Corp. let him go. He chose this job in Kwajalein because he didn't want to sell our farm. We could leave our twenty-year-old son in Tennessee to take care of the farm and pay the bills for us with the money we sent him.

We went to live and work on Kwajalein Island. It was like being on a second honeymoon.

Every Sunday Richard and I would attend church. I was thrilled that he was willing to go to church with me. As I sat in the pew listening to the pastor's sermon, I complained to God: "This man is so boring. I have heard all of this stuff when I was a kid. Doesn't he have anything with depth that he could preach on?"

The Holy Spirit said, *"His sermons aren't for you. They're for your husband."*

"Oh, that's great!" I thought. And I was thrilled to see God's control of everything.

I realized that when we are bored about something, it's best to ask God to help us see things with His eyes. I have used this truth many times since then. We should remember that God encourages us to not complain or grumble. My attitude was being changed, praise God.

God Knows Best

Ephesians 6:8
Knowing that whatever good anyone does, he will
receive the same from the Lord, whether he is a
slave or free.

Richard and I left Kwajalein after only being there a year and a half. We returned to our home in Tennessee, so I could be with my mother in her final days. Time passed and I received a letter from my friend in Kwajalein telling me of the severe storm that came to the island. There was no phone communication; no planes could come in or out. I realized that the hand of God had brought us home before this happened. Otherwise I never would have known of my mother's death. I just stand amazed at how God works his plan into our lives and takes such good care of us.

I want to tell of something I did while I was in Kwajalein that was fun. I worked at the school on the island of Ebay, which is just a few miles by boat from Kwajalein. One thing that the teachers complained about was that whenever they ordered a calendar for their classroom, it was always American things: American presidents, American weather, American holidays, etc. I said, "I know. I will make you a calendar with your holidays and pictures of your beautiful island."

They were thrilled. It was fun being able to help them with a calendar that suited their needs.

I really enjoyed making that calendar for them. When I left the island the calendar was completed and they gave me a beautiful shell vase that they had made for me as a thank you gift. Sea shells are very special to me, so their gift meant a lot and I still have it in my shell collection.

Chapter 4

Our Children

The stories about my children are in
chronological order for each child.
I believe that each story shows the reader the
importance of listening to our children. We can
find wisdom in their words if we just
open our ears to hear.

Volunteering Good or Bad

Colossians 3:21
*Fathers, do not provoke your children, lest they
become discouraged.*

Our children were involved in school
activities and I wanted to volunteer in many of
those activities. It seemed I had a need to be
appreciated. My way of dealing with this need was
to volunteer.

One activity that I really enjoyed was the
Cub Scouts. One year during the summer I
organized a day camp for the Cub Scouts. Our farm
was an ideal place for a fun filled camp. Because of
all my volunteering, I was often too busy to spend
quality time with my own children.

One day my oldest daughter confronted me
with a truth I had never realized. She said, "Mom
why is it that you have all the time to spend with
everyone else's kids but never time to spend with
us?"

I believe God used her to show me I was
letting my need to be appreciated and important to
the community kids outweigh the needs of my own
kids.

I tried to not be so involved from that day
on. One of the ways I tried to change and to satisfy

my daughter's complaint was by sacrificing my time and spending more of it with each of them. I asked my son if there was something he would like me to do with him once a week for fun. He asked if we could play basketball on our basketball court in our backyard. So we set a time and began playing Horse, which was a fun basketball game that could be played by two.

When I asked my youngest daughter how she wanted to spend our time together, she chose for us to cook a meal. We would look through the cookbooks and find something that she liked and then we would cook if for dinner.

Now when I asked my oldest daughter how she wanted to spend our time together, I was truly shocked at how she answered. She said, "I would love for you to not tell me any of your God stories during our time together."

I was once again confronted with the truth. Even a friend had expressed the same thing. Instead of drawing them to God I was pushing them away. God had a lot of work to do on me. I needed God to teach me how to witness to the people I loved. I asked God for His help. He showed me that being a friend to my teenage daughter could be accomplished by listening to her and not lecturing so much. I needed to show more interest in her music, books, and her friends.

Instead of trying to do the work of the Holy Spirit… I should leave it in His hands.

Late-night Episode

Ephesians 5:17
Therefore do not be unwise, but understand what
the will of the Lord is.

Our teenage daughter had begun dating and it was a very hard time for me. She also had been given the use of a sports car that Richard had bought. So I also worried about that. It helped me understand why my father never let me get my driver's license and why my mother sat up until I came home from a date. I decided I would do the same thing.

One particular evening I was waiting for her to come home and as the hours ticked by I became more and more worried. I even began calling the hospital and police department to see if she had been in an accident. Remember, this was long before cell phones.

Then about 3am she drove up and came into the house. I began lecturing her and she gave her defense. Her boyfriend worked nights and she waited until he got off work and then they went to eat. The explanation was not helping the fact that she was treating me so disrespectfully. I told her to go to bed and we would let her dad talk to her in the morning.

The next morning, I told Richard what had happened and ask him to discipline her for her late-night episode. I then took our son to his swim meet, leaving Richard to come to the proper discipline.

You can imagine my surprise when she walked into the swim meet. I was filled with anger and wanted an explanation for how she could have been there.

I said to her, "Did you talk to your father?"

She said yes.

"Well, what did he say your punishment would be for your late-night adventure?"

She replied. "He told me that since I didn't have a rule for a time to be in at night, he was now giving me a curfew. I would now have to be home by 11 o'clock on my nights out."

God gave me peace about the discipline and I was glad that my anger was not the ruling force for my daughter's discipline. Anger was something that God would help me deal with over the years.

Room Mates

Psalm 37:4
Delight yourself also in the Lord, and He shall give
you the desires of your heart.

Our oldest daughter was going to go back to college and wanted her own apartment because she had decided she did not like living in a dorm. We decided to pray and ask God to find her a roommate to help with expenses.

After praying, she came home and said, "Guess what Mom? God has found me two roommates, they are brothers."

I was a little shocked. When she told her Dad, he said, "I'm not worried about the sex part of it, they probably just want you to clean house and cook."

She said, "No way!" but continued to pursue the plan to live with these two brothers.

I was in a dilemma; did I believe God had chosen these two brothers for her roommates? I knew if I said, "No we won't allow you to do that!" she would just rebel and do what she wanted to do. My prayer was for God to be in control of this situation and help me trust Him.

A few days later, a college friend called, she had received a letter from the school telling her there was no room in the dorm for her. She called our daughter and asked if she had an apartment and could they be roommates.

Our daughter said, "Yes, that would be great." Praise God.

A New Job in Colorado

John 14:27
*Peace I leave with you, My peace I give to you; not
as the world gives do I give to you. Let not your
heart be troubled, neither let it be afraid.*

Our oldest daughter had graduated from college and had decided to search for a job in Colorado, a place where we had gone on vacations. She really liked Colorado and decided she wanted to live there. She had an interview with Ball Aerospace for a job as a computer programmer.

When she arrived in Colorado, she called me and said, "Mom, I am really having problems sleeping. I am so nervous. What if I am not really supposed to be here? I have never been this far away from home. I'll be alone. What can I do Mom?"

I told her, "We'll pray and ask God to give you his perfect peace if this is where he wants you to live."

She said, "That will be a miracle, I am so nervous, I can't imagine how He will be able to bring peace to me."

The next morning she called and said, "Mom, I had a beautiful night's rest and I am so peaceful I can't imagine how this happened."

During the interview she had an interesting thing happen. The man who was interviewing her read over her application and said, "Young lady, you have not asked for enough salary. The cost of living in Colorado is much higher than in Tennessee so we need to change the amount you have asked for." She got the job and we moved her into a townhouse not far from work.

She had taken her cat, Patches with her and Patches was very allergic to fleas. It was to the point to where we thought maybe we should put Patches to sleep. We asked God what we needed to do. To our surprise God had gone before us and prepared the way. The salary had been raised, and my daughter's special cat was healed because there were less fleas in Colorado.

We gave thanks and our daughter was confident that God had planned for Colorado to be her new home.

Working With Her Father

Matthew 9:37
... The harvest truly is plentifully, but the laborers are few.

Our second daughter has always had a love for the farm. Even when she was young she liked to spend time with her father taking care of the cattle and helping him with other chores around the farm. Just like I did with my Daddy when I was young.

One particular time a cow was calving and we could see that she was having trouble and would need help, so Richard and our daughter pulled the baby calf from the mother. Our daughter was a great help and enjoyed working on the farm. Every summer we had to cut hay and bail it. The family worked hard putting the hay on the truck and then into the barn.

Another job that had to be done, but that no one liked helping with was harvesting the honey. She even became her father's helper robbing the honey from the bee hives. God used this time to help develop a strong relationship between the two of them.

Don't be Disrespectful

Titus 2:15
You must teach these things and encourage the
believers to do them. You have the authority to
correct them when necessary, so don't let anyone
disregard what you say.

One night our daughter was in the kitchen doing the dishes and her father asked her to bring him a cup of coffee.

"What's the matter you can't walk?" She asked.

"Don't get smart, just bring me my coffee" he said.

She replied, "I just want to ask you a question. If I ask you to bring me a glass of water would you do that for me?"

Richard said, "I am your father and you are to do what I ask you to do."

She said, "Okay but I just wanted to make a point."

She brought him his coffee and we didn't talk about it anymore.

About a week or so later she was in the den doing her homework, and she said, "Oh, shoot!" in disgust. Her father heard her angry remarks, and asked her what the problem was. She told him she needed her math book. He asked her if she had left the math book at school. She told him it was in the car but she didn't want to go out in the cold to get it.

Her father got up from his chair walked outside to the car and got her math book.

I said very calmly, "just say thank you, when he gives you your book, don't be disrespectful. Your father has just shown you an act of kindness. I'm sure your comment last week has prompted him to show you he is willing to do things to show you respect."

Changing Jobs

Hebrews 4:16
Let us therefore come boldly to the throne of grace,
that we may obtain mercy and find grace to help in
time of need.

Our daughter attended Middle Tennessee State University in Murfreesboro. She took art classes and learned a lot about sculpturing and making molds. Her father told her that none of these things she was learning were going to get her a good job. But he was wrong.

Her sister had moved to Colorado and suggested that she come and live with her for a while and try to find a job there in Colorado. She agreed and began looking in the Boulder art community. She found a lady who was a production potter that hired her. We were all thrilled and thought she was settled in a career of art.

The family decided to take a camping vacation in the Colorado mountains. Our trip started out to be a fun adventure but on our last day she slipped on a moss covered rock and injured her wrist. When we arrived home she went to work and found out she was unable to use her hand because of the hurt wrist. Now she had to begin looking for another job. Was this injury God's way of directing her to a new career?

God brought to her mind a young artist that she met at school and he had found work in a dental lab sculpting teeth. She called a dental lab and asked if she could show them her work.

The owner of the lab was impressed with the detail of her sculptures and gave her a job delivering and picking up cases. When she wasn't doing that job she practiced making crowns and learning the techniques for the other procedures in the lab. The owner was very impressed with her ability to   sculpt the crowns and make the wax molds that he gave her and now she had a chance to be an apprentice.

She is still doing this work today where she is using her artistic skills. This injury shows how God uses the bad things as well as the good. God's grace is there for us to help in times of need. Trust Him and come to Him for all of your needs.

Love for the Land

Hebrews 13:16
But do not forget to do good and to share, for with
such sacrifices God is well pleased.

The love of the land was passed on to our daughter from her father. After college she moved to Colorado. She bought her condo and soon after that investment she bought property in the mountains of Colorado. She then bought a travel trailer to have on the property.

During one of our visits to Colorado she and her father built a beautiful deck for the trailer. Her father also taught her how to make decorative Indian ladders from the aspen trees that were on the property. We enjoyed fishing and hiking in the area. The time we spent at the property was always relaxing and peaceful.

Years later after Richard's death she was willing to sell her property and bought a home for her and I to live in. That was a real sacrifice on her part because she loved her land. She has provided me with a beautiful home that we share together.

God has blessed me with children who are willing to love and care for my needs. A few years later she was able to buy another piece of mountain property. The mountains have always given her peace.

Could this be God's Plan?

Roman's 8:28
And we know that all things work together for good
to those who love God, to those who are the called
according to His purpose.

Our son was six years younger than his older sister. He didn't develop his asthma problems until we moved to the farm in Tennessee, when he was seven. There were many things on the farm that he was allergic to, which caused his asthma problems. Around age 8 or 9, our son was having trouble with his breathing. When his friends would come over, they would want to go swimming in the creek. But his breathing was such a problem that I would have to carry him down to the creek.

After playing in the cool water for about an hour, he was able to walk by himself up the hill with no breathing problems. We praised God, and this lead us to believe that maybe he should join the swim team. This did not heal his asthma but it was helpful.

God Answers the Prayers of Little Children

James 5:17
...He prayed earnestly that it would not rain and it did not rain...

At one of our son's swim meets, it was raining with thunder and lightning. The kids could not get in the water. As we sat waiting for the storm to pass, our son told his little friend sitting next to him, "If my Mommy will pray and ask God, the storm will go away."

I was under pressure. I told the boys, "You don't need me to pray, you can do it yourself." They both bowed their heads and asked God to take away the storm.

Guess what? Their prayers were answered and the swim meet continued! God doesn't always answer prayers this quickly, but on this day He did. My children learned the importance of prayer and we lived a life filled with praises to God for answered prayers.

Don't Sleep in Your Armor

Ephesians 6:11,14-18
Put on the whole armor of God,that you may be
able to stand against the wiles of the devil.
Stand therefore, having gird your waist with truth,
having put on the breastplate of righteousness, and
having shod your feet with the preparation of the
gospel of peace; above all, taking the shield of faith
with which you will be able to quench all the fiery
darts of the wicked one. And take the helmet of
salvation, and the sword of the Spirit, which is the
word of God. Praying always with all prayer and
supplication in the Spirit.

I had taught my children the importance of putting on their whole armor of God each morning for protection. This is not just something that children should do, but it should be used by everybody. I continue to wear my armor every day.

One particular morning our son came to the breakfast table and he was grumpy.

"What's the matter with you?" I asked.

"I didn't sleep very good," he said.

"Why?"

"I forgot to take my armor off!" he said as we both laughed

Healing Came in the Night

Matthew 21:22
And whatever things you ask in prayer, believing,
you will receive.

One night I was getting ready to go to bed and I walked by the table where my ten year old son was doing his homework and he was wheezing and having a very hard time breathing. Usually I would have him lay down on the couch and I would rub his back and his chest to help him to relax. Sometimes it would help and sometimes it wouldn't.

This time as I walked by him the Holy Spirit said *"Go to bed, leave him with Me."* I told my son goodnight, and that the Holy Spirit would help him. He gasped and begged me to stay with him. I told him I was sorry but I couldn't.

I went to bed and I told the Lord, "If you don't put me to sleep immediately I am going back to my son to help him." To my surprise, I fell quickly to sleep.

The next morning, I asked my son, "What happened last night?"

"Right after you left me, the wheezing stopped and I knew God had touched my body," he said.

We were so pleased and we praised God. It didn't work like that every night, but that was the night that God wanted to show us His power.

God was Preparing the Way

John 14:27
... Let not your heart be troubled, neither let it be afraid.

Since our son had such problems breathing, his pediatrician suggested we take him to see an allergist. They put him on allergy shots. After some time there really wasn't much improvement so we came to the conclusion this really was not the answer to his asthma problem. So the pediatrician said he was going to try and find a clinic that could find the root of the problem. We were praying for God's help but the answer didn't seem to be coming.

Every week the nurse at the allergist's office would send the medicine to the pediatrician's office so that our son could receive his allergy shot. For some reason one month the medicine never made it to the pediatrician's office. So our son was without his allergy shots for almost a month. When we went to see the pediatrician and told him what was happening, he said, "That is perfect."

The Denver Asthma Clinic, where he had signed our son up, said that before he could be seen he had to be off his medication for one month. God was going before us and preparing the way.

Wisdom

Isaiah 41:10
Fear not, for I am with you; be not dismayed, for I
am your God. I will strengthen you, yes, I will help
you, I will uphold you with My righteous right hand.

Now we had to start making plans to get our
son to Denver, Colorado. One night we discussed
the trip and my husband said, "The two of you will
drive to Denver, Colorado."

In an angry manner our son said, "No, I
want to fly!"

His father said, "This is my decision, and
you are going to take the car."

Our son became hysterical and ran into his
bedroom. I was close behind him. When I asked
our son to explain why he was being so adamant, he
asked me, "Do you know where all the hospitals are
from here to Colorado? If I need to have a
breathing treatment, can you get me there quick?"

I got up; walked into the kitchen and told
my husband what had caused our son to be so
worried and upset. We thought he was acting this
way because he wanted to fly on an airplane. I was
so thankful that I had asked him to explain. His
wisdom was truly from God. My Husband said,
"Get the tickets tomorrow for your flight to
Denver."

Secure in the Arms of God

Psalm 91:11
For He shall give His angels charge over you, to
keep you in all your ways.

The next morning after the doctor told us
that he had found an asthma clinic in Denver,
Colorado, where my son could go for treatment God
brought to my mind a family who now lived in
Colorado. They were neighbors of ours years ago.
They had moved to Colorado Springs. It seemed
like the Holy Spirit wanted me to call them. So I
did.

To my surprise, my friend said, "We've
been thinking about you, what's happening?" So I
told her the whole story.

She said, "If you will fly into Colorado
Springs, I will pick you up and drive you to the
clinic in Denver."

I thanked her for being so helpful and I
became making our plans for the trip. I had no idea
they needed me as much as I needed them and God
was calling me out there for a reason.

After we arrived, and caught up what had
happened in our lives since we last saw each other,
everything *seemed* to be going fine for both our
families.

The next morning, we left for the Denver Asthma Clinic. When we arrived, my friend told me she would come and pick me up when I was ready. Once my son was settled in, I was ready for her to come back and pick me up.

When we were back in Colorado Springs, they shared with me the problems that they were having with their business. We prayed about each of these problems. And soon God gave us solutions for each of them. He was shocked but knew that it was God's power that was helping him. He told me before I left that he would never walk away from God again.

Finding Help in a New City

Philippians 4:7
And the peace of God, which surpasses all
understanding, will guard your hearts and minds
through Christ Jesus.

Our ten-year-old son was going to be living at the Denver Asthma Clinic for an undetermined amount of time while he received treatment for his asthma. After admitting him to the clinic, they told me of a lady who would open her home to the family of patients so they could stay close to the clinic. It would be of no charge. This was a perfect plan and I called the lady and got directions to her home. I visited her home and it was just a short distance from the clinic and the room was perfect for my needs. While our son would be staying at the clinic for treatment I wanted him to attend church. The lady recommended a church that was within walking distance from the clinic.

So we attended services there that next Sunday. After the services, they had a time for fellowship. We walked back to the fellowship hall and talked to the members about how my son was going to be staying at the asthma clinic until they could find a treatment for his asthma.

One lady told me, "We drive by the asthma clinic on our way to church. We would love to pick up your son and bring him to church with us while he is staying at the clinic." With that settled I knew God had helped us one more time.

Trust and Obey

Acts 3:19
Repent therefore and be converted, that your sins
may be blotted out, so that times of refreshing may
come from the presence of the Lord.

This story shows how the Holy Spirit prepares the
way for His work to be accomplished.

The next day I was to talk with one of the
nurses at the clinic about my son's treatment. That
morning before I left for the clinic, the Holy Spirit
spoke to me and said, *"You will meet **Epi** and she
will confess her sins. You will pray with her to
accept Jesus."*

My comment back to the Holy Spirit was, "I
don't know Epi."

And His response was, *"Trust and Obey."*

When I got to the clinic I went to the desk
and asked, "What do you have planned for me
today?"

She said, "One moment please, let me call
Epi, she's the nurse that will be training you on how
you can help your son with the treatment of his
asthma."

Wow! I couldn't believe that I was going to meet Epi.

I told God, "I don't mind telling her what you want me to tell her, and I don't mind listening to her sins but she has to bring it up to me."

I spent the whole day with her and not once did we talk about sins. At the end of the day, I went down stairs to the lobby and was going to call a cab. The elevator door opened and to my surprise, Epi stepped into the lobby.

She said, "Oh, I am so glad you haven't left yet."

I said, "Is there anything wrong?"

She replied, "Oh no, no. I just wanted to talk to you. You seem like someone I can trust."

We sat down in the lobby and she told me about her life. I told her about Jesus and prayed for her to receive His gift of forgiveness. She cried and thanked me.

Chapter 5

My Parents

I am very thankful that God showed His mercy to me by His role as the Great Physician to my parents. God also blessed me by letting me be a part of my Mother's acceptance of Jesus.

Richard Has Some Good Advice

Ephesians 2:1-2
And you He made alive, who were dead in
trespasses and sins, in which you once walked
according to the course of this world ...

When we had moved to Tennessee the kids were teenagers and we decided it would be fun to drive to Indiana to spend Christmas with the family. It was a fun time for the kids playing with my sister's children. They were all about the same age.

But unfortunately my mother was her usual negative self and said many things about our children that caused me to be very angry.

When we left I was alone with Richard in the cab of our truck. I began spilling all my anger out to him, I said, "I will never come back to see my mother again! She is so awful."

Richard's comment was, "She is your mother and you will forgive her."

I knew he was right, so with God's help I forgave my mother and I put that incident behind us.

Reconciliation didn't come right away. Time passed and on one of my parents visits to our home. I was able to share God's healing of memories with my mother. Praise God!

The Truth is Spoken

Colossians 4:6
Let your speech always be with grace, seasoned
with salt, that you may know how you ought answer
each one.

My mother and father would visit us on the
farm and usually stay for a month. This was very
hard on our family because my mother was very
negative. She would say upsetting things about my
father, my husband, and my children. I definitely
needed help.

I went for a walk and cried out to God and
asked Him what I needed to do. He brought the
thought to me that *I should tell my mother the truth.*
But I told the Lord that I didn't know what the truth
was. When I came back from my walk I found my
Mother in the kitchen.

"Mother I need to tell you something," I
said. "If you don't stop saying hateful negative
things about the ones I love you are not going to
come and visit us ever again."

She looked stunned and told me I couldn't
do that. I promptly told her that this was God's
truth not mine. From that moment on when she
started to talk I would say, "Mother, have you
thought about what you are going to say?" She
would shake her head and walk away so she
wouldn't say anything negative.

God Takes Care of My Father

Psalm 118:17
I shall not die, but live, and declare the works of the Lord.

When the kids were old enough to stay by themselves, I found out that my father had a tumor in his stomach the size of a grapefruit. My mother called and asked if I would come and be with him and I was thankful that I was free to do that. They were going to put Daddy in the hospital and operate to remove the tumor. I told her "Of course I would come".

I called my church and asked if they would please pray for my father. I headed for Indiana, a seven-hour trip. It was a time of singing and praising God and praying for my father's healing.

When I arrived, my father's friends and family had come to visit him. I told them, "If you want to see my father, you can come in if you promise to speak only loving words and tell him happy things. Nothing negative allowed. If you can't do this, don't come in."

The next morning, my sister, mother and I were waiting for the doctor's report. When he came, he said he had some good news. The tumor is gone. My sister, mother and I praised the Lord and knew that God had taken care of my father.

Who Was Disrespectful?

Proverbs 19:20
Listen to counsel and receive instruction that you
may be wise in your latter days.

My mother and father were visiting us on the farm and I felt that we should ask my father for advice since he had been a farmer all of his life, and a very good one. We had some cattle that we were going to sell and Richard said to me, "Take them over to the sale barn and leave them for Tuesday's sale."

My father made the suggestion, "Why don't we just take them early Tuesday morning rather than leave them at the sale barn all night? It might make them nervous and they might even lose weight leaving them there."

To my surprise, Richard said, "No, we'll take them Monday night like I said."

I was crushed.

I followed Richard into the house and I said, "Why did you treat my father so disrespectfully?"

He said, "I didn't. It's my farm, my cattle, and I'll do it the way I want to. That's not disrespect. He's showing me disrespect by telling me how to run my farm."

He went to work leaving me to help my father load the cattle. I told my father how sorry I was that Richard didn't want to do it his way.

My gracious father said, "It's ok, this is his farm and he must do things the way he sees to do them, not the way I see."

When we took the cattle to the sale barn, they had us back up to a loading shoot that went into a beautiful big pen, probably 15 x 15, with a trough for water and another for feed, and an entrance into a grassy area where they could graze. This area belonged to them, their own special space! I knew Richard was right and our cows were well taken care of while they were at the Sale Barn and probably wouldn't lose any weight.

My father said, "I've never seen an arrangement like this in a cattle barn before!"

Neither had I. So we all learned a lesson that day.

My Mother Accepts Jesus

Ephesians 2:8
For by grace you have been saved through faith,
and that not of yourselves; it is the gift of God.

One visit from my parents was a true blessing. The church I attended was having a woman's retreat so I signed up my mother and myself to attend. When my parents arrived I told my mother that I had signed her up to attend the retreat. She informed me that she didn't want to do that and I told her that was fine. She could stay at home and take care of the kids and cook for the family. This changed her mind so she told me that she would go to the retreat with me.

When we got to the retreat, I signed my mother and I into different classes. I didn't want to hinder the work of the Holy Spirit. The prompting of the Holy Spirit proved to be right, praise God.

When the class was over a friend of mine who was in my mother's class came over to me and whispered in my ear. "Your mother accepted Jesus."

For the rest of the retreat I saw a beautiful change come over my mother. When we got home she was singing and was loving and kind to the family. The kids asked me what happened to Grandma, and I told them she had accepted Jesus to be her savior.

Richard also asked me what had happened to my mother. I told him she accepted Jesus. His comment was: "she should have done that a long time ago!" What a blessing we all received.

My Father's Illness

Each time a loved one became ill, I was given the privilege of spending time with them in their hour of need. The one that impressed me the most was my father's tumor that God healed miraculously. His kidney failure was the illness that taught me the greatest lesson about taking care of the elderly who were ill. This was more serious than his tumor. Dad seemed to know he was soon to meet his Maker. He had kidney failure and did not want to go on the dialysis machine. He said that he wanted to die at home.

My mother asked my brother, sister and me if we would take turns helping her take care of Dad. When it came my turn, I told Mother that I would take the night shift so she could sleep and get some rest.

My dad did not want to take his medicine, didn't want anybody to help him do anything, and was really very belligerent. For example, I'd put the pill in his mouth and he'd spit it back at me.

I asked God, "Why do you keep my father here? He's ready to go and be with Jesus. Give me a Scripture that will help me understand what's happening in his life."

The Scripture that came to me was, *"I was hungry and you fed me. I was thirsty and you gave me drink."*

I stopped the Holy Spirit. "That doesn't pertain to this situation! I want a Scripture that pertains to my father now."

The answer came back, *"Your father was thirsty, and you gave him drink. Your father was hungry, and you fixed his favorite meal. Your father was naked, and you dressed him. Your father was a prisoner in his own home and you came to visit him. Your father has become the least of the brethren, and what you do unto him, you do as unto Me. Serve Me well."*

Now it all made sense. God was giving us the opportunity to serve Him in love through my father. When I was prompted, I told this to other people going through similar situations with their ill family members. It helped make sense as to why the elderly and the ill are kept here so we can serve Jesus in love.

My Mother's Illness

Romans 12:2
Do not be conformed to this world, but be
transformed by the renewing of your mind, that you
may prove what is that good and acceptable and
perfect will of God.

While we were in Kwajalein, my mother became very ill, and I felt very frustrated that I was so far from her. My husband arranged for us to have a sabbatical so that I could go and visit my mother for two weeks.

Of course my mother was excited, thinking that I was going to be home for good. I told her, "No, Mom, this is only for two weeks."

She replied, "Couldn't you ask Richard to let you stay here?"

My response to her was: "we'll ask God."

When I prayed and asked God if I could stay, He told me, "*I have not chosen you to take care of your mother.*"

When I went back the next day to see my mother, I didn't know how she was going to receive what I had to tell her. I said, "Mom, I asked God if I could stay with you and he told me..." and before I could finish she said, "I know, He told me, too, but we've had this nice time together, haven't we?"

Richard and I returned to Kwajalein, and I told God, "If you let anything happen to my mother while I'm out here on this island, I'll be very mad."

Richard knew the pain that I was feeling, and he came home one afternoon with some unbelievable news: "I've lost my job."

"Praise the Lord!" I said.

"I knew you would be happy," Richard said.

Now we began packing up to leave Kwajalein and return to our home in Tennessee.

When we returned from Kwajalein I went to visit Mom for a while. Since it was Thanksgiving I told Mom that I was going to go home and have Thanksgiving. Then I would come back and visit her again.

"Can you please pray for me to die?" She asked.

"Mom, I can't do that!" I replied.

"Do you love me?" She asked.

"Yes, but I don't want you to die?"
"My bone cancer is so painful, and I have no real purpose or reason to live. I just want to die."

I took her hand and prayed that God's will would be done in her life.

I went back to Tennessee to have Thanksgiving with my family, and the day after Thanksgiving we got a phone call that my mother had passed away. I should have been very sad, but I felt that God had worked this plan for her and it made me happy that she had received her request.

After I received the message that my mother had died, I went to the Sunday evening church service at my current church; the pastor asked if there was anybody who needed prayer.

I stood up and said, "My mother has just passed away, and I would like prayer for our family."

I sat back down. The pastor didn't pray. No one said anything to me. It was bizarre. It was like they didn't even hear me. The end of the service came and I thought surely someone would come over to comfort me, but no one did. It was as if I wasn't even there.

I left the church, and when I got into the car, I broke down and I said to God, "I don't understand what's happening. I need you to comfort me."
I thought my church was where I could find comfort.

The Holy Spirit said to me, *"I have chosen who you need to comfort you."*

When I arrived home, Richard said, "Sue and Mary both have called you."

They both had lost their mothers and were very comforting to me in my hour of need. God always knows best!

Chapter 6

Soni

Soni came into my life to teach me how God works, if we yield to Him. I wanted to walk with the Holy Spirit and trust His leadership. Soni had lived a very hard life and she needed help believing God could use her. The Holy Spirit taught both of us how wonderful your life could be if you walked with His help.

God's Appointed Bible Study

Ephesians 4:2 (NLT)
Always be humble and gentle. Be patient with each
other, making allowance for each other's faults
because of Your love.

In my prayer time I had been asking God to let me meet someone of his choosing that could mentor me. If there was a bible study that I might be able to attend, and he brought into my mind a young lady that I had met once. I called her and asked what she was doing and she said she was teaching a Bible Study. It just happened to be a few miles from my home. So I asked her if I could come and she was glad to have me.

The first day that I attended was very interesting. One of the ladies was named Soni. I had never met her before and it just so happened that she had just tried to kill herself. As she told the story of that event I was praying and asking God to help me know what to do.

The leader said to Soni "Ok pray this prayer."

Soni responded, "I have prayed that prayer many times with you and nothing happens".

The leader stood up and said to the group: "Let's go out on the front porch and ask God what he wants us to do with Soni."

Everyone followed her, but I sat in my seat. She turned around and said to me, "Are you coming?"

I said, "No I already know what God wants me to do."

I was discerning that the leader of this bible study was not someone I wanted to study with. I felt she did not have the compassion of Christ that I wanted in my life. I felt no compassion from her for this woman who was in pain. I saw that she looked disgusted with me, not compassionate. She said nothing else and walked outside.

I said to Soni, "Can you say this prayer with me?"
"Father create in my heart love for my husband, love for my children, and love for myself."

She began to cry and said, "Oh yes, I want that more than anything."

Then she prayed the most beautiful prayer I have ever heard. Truly her heart belonged to Jesus. Little did I know that Soni was the one God chose to disciple me. I learned so many things from this beautiful lady.

The other ladies came back in and I told them that Soni and I were going to leave. I took her in my car and we drove to her house. When we got to her house I asked her if she would like to have a bible study just her and I? She said that sounded wonderful.

My New Friend

Psalm 25:4-5
Show me Your ways, O Lord; Teach me Your paths.
Lead me in Your truth and teach me, for You are the
God of my salvation; on You I wait all the day.

My new friend, Soni was married and had
three sons. When we came to her home she
introduced me to her husband, Tom. I told him that
Soni and I were going to study the bible together
and he asked if he could join us. I said that would
be fine and we planned to begin the next
Wednesday.

As I prepared for the study I realized that
they had not even asked me what we were going to
study, but as we began talking about different
passages in the bible and about Jesus, I realized they
had many misconceptions. I might have gotten in
over my head.

The first thing that happened was her
husband decided that he would let the two of us
study and he went on about his business and he left
us to study by ourselves. Since Soni and I had never
met before I decided to ask her about her life and
why she had wanted to kill herself. She told me that
she had epilepsy and the seizures were getting more
intense and her medicine did not seem to be
working.

Did She Have Demons?

Zechariah 4:6
... This is the word of the Lord to Zerubbabel; it is not by power, nor by might, but by My Spirit says the Lord of hosts.

The church Soni attended had told her that she probably needed to be delivered from the demons that were in her. I was amazed.

I asked her, "Soni what happens if you are delivered and you still have seizures, then what would be the next step?" She said she would cross that bridge when she came to it.

She told me the date she was going to be delivered at the church and she asked if I would go with her. I was rather reluctant, but I agreed. I had never been a part of a deliverance team but I agreed to go with her.

When we arrived at the church she introduced me to her pastor and he said, "Yes, I've heard about you and I would rather you not be present."

I was relieved and so I said, "That will be fine. I will wait in the Sanctuary." I prayed and wept and asked God for His will to be accomplished.

Soni came out, and she looked very tired. We got in the car and I said let's go have lunch. We stayed in the car to eat our lunch and as she sat there eating she just began taking the food and jamming it into her mouth, while she made strange sounds.

I just sat there and said, "Thank you Jesus. Thank you Jesus."

She quietly finished her lunch and said, "What happened?"

I said, "I don't know, but it's ok now."

Sometime later, Soni and I invited her husband Tom to go out to lunch with us. We were sitting at the table eating and Soni stiffened and starting making those sounds again. I took her hand and starting saying, "Thank you Jesus. Thank you Jesus."

She stopped, sat up straight and said "what happened?"

Her husband said, "You just had a seizure!"

Then he looked at me and asked, "How did you do that?'

"How did I do what?" I replied.

"Make it go away?" He said.

"I didn't do anything, it was Jesus that made it go away," I answered.

Soni asked me one day, "Do you know why you met me?"

"No, why?" I answered.

"Because my life is hell and God wanted you to see what hell was like," she told me. "And He gave you the power to help me live in God's kingdom."

Finding a New Doctor

Hebrews 4:16
Let us therefore come boldly to the throne of grace,
that we may obtain mercy and find grace to help in
time of need.

Soni was in need of another doctor. She asked me if I could help her select one. It is very important when making decisions for your life to ask God for His help. So I asked God to bring to my understanding what He wanted her to do. When I was looking in the telephone book, I noticed that one of the doctors was in an area close to Soni's home. I felt God was directing me to this doctor, so I made an appointment and took Soni to see him.

Soni asked me to go into the doctor's office with her, and I agreed. I explained to him everything that I was aware of that I thought was unusual. He asked her what medicine she was on and started to look at her records. He gave us an explanation that sounded reasonable: The medicine she was taking had built up in her system and was causing her to have seizures rather than helping her.

He was a very compassionate man and said he would like to work with Soni and I agreed to bring her to see him again. It is so important to seek God first in all decisions. I remembered in James 1:5, it tells us to ask God for wisdom, so I was happy to ask.

Victory!

James 4:7
Therefore submit to God. Resist the devil and he
will flee from you.

Soni had three sons and they were all teenagers. They needed a lot of discipline and neither her husband nor Soni were really capable of bringing them to a place of being obedient. These boys were not her husband's sons, so they did not respect him. They would not do what he told them to do. They were belligerent and caused fights and they were really much bigger than Tom. They could easily overpower him.

Soni asked me to pray and I told her I had been. I told her when they began fighting she was to pray, "In the name of Jesus, I command you Satan to get your hands off my family!"

She said she would try. A few days later she called me and I could hear the boys screaming and yelling. I could hear things being broken. Soni was crying and said, "I forgot what the prayer was!"

I reminded her of the prayer and I advised her to hang up, go into the living room, and take authority over this fight. I dropped to my knees and began praying that Jesus would give Soni victory over the situation. A little bit later Soni called and said, "It worked!" I praised God for the victory.

Sins Have Been Forgiven

Ephesians 1:7
In Christ we have redemption through His blood,
the forgiveness of sins, according to the riches of
His grace.

As I was driving to Soni's house one day the Holy Spirit said, *"Tell Soni that her sins, past, present and future have been forgiven."*

I thought to myself, *"Father I am sorry, but I am not sure I believe that."*

He responded, *"Trust me, it's the truth."*

I went into Soni's house and said, "Soni I have something to tell you from God, your sins past, present and future have been forgiven."

She looked surprised and said, "Are you sure?"
I looked her straight in the eye and said, "Yes it is the truth!" God's grace was setting her free.

Soni never talked about her sins but she asked me to show her what to read in the Bible that could help her believe what I had just told her. I decided it would be a good idea to have a Bible study to research that. I realized that I needed to know where I could find this truth.

Soni Prayed for My Healing

Mark 11:24
Therefore I say to you, whatever things you ask
when you pray, believe that you receive them and
you will have them.

One day I woke up with a very stiff neck, so
I decided to call Soni and tell her I couldn't come
for bible study. Then the idea came to me to ask
my son to drive me to Soni's. He agreed and when
we pulled up in front of Soni's house the Holy
Spirit said, *"Ask Soni to pray for your healing."*

My thought was, "Soni? You want Soni to
pray for my healing?"

Okay.

When I got inside of the house I told her
about my stiff neck and I asked her to please lay
hands on my neck and pray for me to be healed.

"I can't do that!" She said.

I replied, "Soni I think whatever you ask, it
will be done!"

"Okay," She said.

She put her hands on my neck and prayed
for healing. Guess what? The stiffness left and the
pain was gone.

Soni said, "God hears my prayers. He answers me!"

From that day forward Soni began praying for her sons' salvation. Two of her sons, received Jesus and we are still praying for her youngest son's salvation.

God Planned My Trip

James 4:15
*Instead you ought to say, if the Lord wills, we shall
live and do this or that.*

My daughter that lived in Colorado wanted
me to visit her. I went to visit with Soni before I left
and the Holy Spirit prompted *me to invite Soni to go
with me.*

I said "Please Father, I don't want the
responsibility of watching over her, because of her
seizures."

The answer was *"Trust me."*

When I got inside of the house I began
telling Soni about my trip.

"Where does your daughter live?" She asked
me

"Louisville, Colorado," I told her.

"Really?" she asked. "My sister lives in
Louisville, Colorado!"

Now I understood. So I asked if she would
like to go with me, so that she could visit her sister.
She said she would like that and she was sure her
sister would be happy to have her visit.

"Yes Lord" I prayed. "Now I understand."

When will I except God's commands the first time He asks me? God, forgive me for always being hesitant.

God Sent Soni to Help Me

James 5:16
*Confess your trespasses to one another, and pray
for one another, that you may be healed. The
effective, fervent prayer of a righteous man avails
much.*

My mother was sick and needed an
operation to have one of her kidneys removed. I was
praying and asking God to help me through this
trial. I had just ended my prayer when my dear
friend Soni drove up.

"Is there anything wrong?" She asked. "I felt
you needed help."

"Yes, I need your prayers" I answered.

She took me in her arms and prayed for me.
I felt the compassion and love of Christ just flow
over me. I thanked Him for sending her to help me.
I asked her to pray for my mother's healing and
then the next day I left to be with my mother and
family with confidence that God would bring His
will to pass in her life. The operation was a success
and we praised God.

Soni Helps Again

After Richard's death I was very lonely and felt that I had no purpose in my life. Soni came again to my aid.

She came to my house and just held me while I cried. I laid down on the couch and we began to talk about life and death. Her husband had died from lung cancer a few months ago.

As I laid on the couch the Holy Spirit prompted me to ask Soni if she would like to come and live with me. She thought that would be wonderful so we began to make plans to move her from Alabama to Tennessee.

I felt so thankful that I would have someone to study the bible with, pray with, and cook with. It was going to be great and I was looking forward to having her move in.

Finding a Tennessee Doctor for Soni

Psalm 91:10-11
No evil shall befall you. Nor shall any plague come near your dwelling; for He shall give His angels charge over you. To keep you in all your ways.

Now that Soni was living with me in Tennessee, we had to find another doctor for her. I don't remember how I found the doctor, but it amazed me to find out that this doctor had done her dissertation on epilepsy! Wasn't that great how God led us to find this doctor for Soni?

Soni was still having seizures and had fallen down the stairs once, but the seizures were not as bad as they had been in the past.

I sat in with Soni as she talked to the doctor and helped to tell her history. The doctor told us that Soni needed to have her medicine changed again. She would have to be taken off of it gradually. In my mind I thought she would be put in the hospital for this procedure, but the doctor informed me that her insurance would not pay for that. The doctor assured me that I could help her through this and that we could call her any time, morning, noon or night if I needed help.

Soni agreed she wanted to do this and we got instructions from the doctor. The doctor told us that the seizures would become very intense as the medicine was taken away. Needless to say, I prayed for Jesus to help us.

Finally, she was completely free from the medicine. When the doctor put her on the new medicine Soni felt much better. Praise God for the new doctor and medicine.

My Move to Colorado

Proverbs 20:24
A man's steps are of the Lord; how then can a man
understand his own way?

I decided to move to Colorado, because both of my girls were living there and I wanted to be near them. My unmarried daughter, bought a house perfect for us to live in together. But we had a problem: where would Soni go?

We found low-income housing for people that needed assistance but they were fully occupied. The only way for someone to get housing there was for someone to die or leave.

"I am not going to pray for someone to die." I told Soni, and instead we prayed for someone to leave.

Not long after that prayer, a woman decided to go live with her daughter. It opened up a duplex. These were really nice units. They had a kitchen, living room, bedroom and bath and each room had a cord to pull telling the office you needed help. They would call each morning and ask if you had a restful night. They would call at night to see if you needed anything before you went to bed. Soni loved it and met lots of nice people. God took care of Soni and worked out all the details. Praise God. Now I was free to move to Colorado to start my new life.

Chapter 7

Miracles

Every day we experience miracles, but many don't believe anything supernatural ever took place. I claim God to be the source of miracles and by sharing these stories I glorify Him. I pray that through my stories I will help people to believe and gain a relationship with Christ and begin to see the miracles in their lives.

Did God Send Me an Angel?

Philippians 4:6-7
Be anxious for nothing, but in everything by prayer and supplication, with thanksgiving, let your requests be made known to God and the peace of God, which surpasses all understanding, will guard your hearts and minds through Christ Jesus.

When my girls were four and two I traveled from California to my Mom and Dad's home in Indiana. I chose this bus trip because I was not going to need to change buses. I was happy to set up camp on the bus and not have to worry about changing buses with my young girls.

Not long after our trip began, the bus was having mechanical problems. So guess what? I had to get off the bus with all my stuff and two little girls. I got into the bus station and found a seat for us and waited. They explained to us that there would be other buses to transport us to our destination, but with only a few empty seats. It would be first come, first served. We would have to go and find a seat on another bus on our own.

Each time a bus would arrive, I would gather up all my stuff and my two little girls. When I would arrive at the door of the bus the bus driver would say, "Sorry lady, no more seats".

This happened three times. I finally prayed, "God please help me!" I sat back down with tears rolling down my cheeks. I knew God was going to work this out, but how? This is how God took action: I believe he sent us an angel.

A man came up to me and said, "Lady, stay right here. I will get you a seat on the next bus."

He did and we were able to ride that bus all the way to Indianapolis, Indiana. Praise God for my angel.

Peace Brother

James 5:16
*...The effective, fervent prayer of a righteous man
avails much.*

We were now living in Tennessee and our
children were old enough to take care of
themselves, so I decided to take a bus to visit my
parents. During this trip I had an interesting
experience. The bus arrived in Nashville and the
driver told us that we needed to get off, because it
was going to be cleaned and serviced. I went
inside, found a seat and sat down.

There was a man sitting across from me
reading his paper and his legs were extended out in
front of him. A gentleman came walking down the
aisle and tripped over the other man's feet. This
made the one who tripped mad, and he went up to
the seated man and cursed at him. He was a strong
man and he grabbed the other man from his seat and
lifted him up.

I thought, I better get out of here, there is
going to be a fight! But the Holy Spirit said *stay
and pray*.

So I prayed fervently asking God to work
his power of forgiveness into these men who were
so angry. I was amazed at how quickly God began
to work.

The larger man sat the smaller man down in his seat and let go of him. It seemed like God was performing a miracle before my very eyes. God had softened the larger man's heart and it showed in his expression.

He reached out his hand and they shook hands and he said, "Peace Brother".

I wanted to go up and say, "Do you know God just touched you?", but I left good enough alone and praised Him myself.

Dolly, Where Are You?

1Thessalonian 5:16-18
Rejoice always, pray without ceasing, in everything
give thanks; for this is the will of God in Christ
Jesus for you.

I was going to visit my parents in Indiana and I was taking the bus again. The bus was much nicer than driving since I didn't like travelling alone in the car. I boarded the bus and found a seat in front of a mother and her child. After a short while, the little girl began crying. My thought was, this is going to be a long trip.

I decided this was a good place to invite God to come and help. I asked Him to quiet the little girl and let the mother have a loving attitude towards her child. The first thing that happened was the mother's attitude changed.

Instead of rudely talking to the little girl and telling her to shut up, she asked, "What are you crying about?" in a very loving manner.

The little girl sobbed and said, "I can't find my dolly".

"I think I know where your dolly is", the mother said.
She found the dolly, gave it to her daughter, and we had a peaceful trip.

I continue to this day to send the Holy Spirit to minister peace to young children when they are crying and fretful. God cares about everything and helps when we call on Him.

God Makes Me a New Schedule

Colossians 1:10
That you may walk worthy of the Lord, fully
pleasing Him, being fruitful in every good work and
increasing in the knowledge of God

Our church at Christmas time would go to a nursing home to visit and sing songs to the residents.

"This makes me sad," I said to my friend.

"What are you talking about?" she asked.

"Well, these people need us more than just at Christmas time. It just upsets me that people only come once a year," I replied.

Her response to me was, "Well, come back more often."

"I am too busy," I said. "I don't have time."

"Well, neither does anyone else." she said.

This pointed out something to pray about. I told God I was willing to go to the nursing home more often if He would help me fit it into my schedule.

Guess what? He made it possible for me to go three days a week.

Giving a Helping Hand

Ephesians 2:10
For we are His workmanship, created in Christ
Jesus for good works, which God prepared before
hand, that we should walk in them.

After God miraculously rearranged my schedule I began visiting some of the residents at the nursing home three times a week. I got to know some of them very well.

One resident that I remember fondly was Mrs. Knolls. She was a beautiful Christian lady, but in lots of physical pain because of her arthritis. I had the privilege of answering her correspondence for her. She would dictate and I would write the letters to friends and family.

This was a delight and brought me joy to feel that I was doing something useful to help her.

Another Special Lady

Mark 10:27
*Jesus looked at them and said, "With men it is
impossible, but not with God; for with God all
things are possible."*

I met another lady at the nursing home.
Eunice, was what you might call a lukewarm
Christian.

In our conversation one day, she said, "God
has never done anything for me."

"Oh, Eunice!" I said. "How can you say
that? He gives you air to breathe, a place to live,
and children that love you. What more could you
ask for?"

"I mean something big, like a miracle!"
Eunice answered.

"Ok, God, we want a miracle for Eunice!" I
said.

I can't remember when, or how long it was
before God performed Eunice's miracle but one day
I came into the nursing home and found Eunice in a
wheelchair. This was very unusual, because she was
very capable of walking on her own. I asked her
what happened.

"I have gangrene in my foot," she said.
"And they are going to amputate it tomorrow."

"Oh no" I said. "May I see your foot?" I took her slipper off and her toes were all black and smelly.

"Can I ask my church to pray for you tonight?" I asked her.

"I think it is too late!" She replied.

I bent over, kissed her toe and put her slipper back on and said, "Let's go see Mrs. Knolls."

Mrs. Knolls' room was just down the hall. When we got there, Mrs. Knolls was surprised to see Eunice in a wheelchair and asked what the problem was. Eunice explained about having gangrene in her foot and that they were going to amputate her foot tomorrow.

Mrs. Knolls asked, "Can I see your foot?" I bent over and took her slipper off and the toes were nice and pink.

"Oh, I took the wrong slipper off!" I said.

When I took the other slipper off, those toes were also pink! God had given her a miracle! The three of us praised the Lord for this healing.

The next day, when I went to see Eunice, everybody was sitting with their feet up. I asked why they were doing that. The doctor said that it

118

helped Eunice's circulation and healed her foot, so the doctor told them all to keep their feet up. I realized the doctor didn't believe in miracles. How sad. But the three of us knew that it was God who had worked the miracle.

One of God's Prayer Warriors

Ephesians 6:18
Praying always with all prayer and supplication in
the Spirit, being watchful to this end with all
perseverance, and supplication for all the saints.

I went to visit my friend, Mrs. Knolls and
she wasn't in her room. I asked the nurse where she
was and found out that she'd been sent to the
hospital. I went to the hospital to visit her there.
When I arrived, a nurse told me what room my
friend was in.

"I don't believe she will be with us through
the night," she told me. "She will be gone by
morning. She's in a coma now."

I went into her room, pulled a chair up to her
bed and began to sing Scripture songs. Also, I felt
it was important to pray in the Spirit for her.

I really don't know how long I stayed, but I
stood up at the end of my songs and I said to her,
"I'll be back tomorrow and we'll go for a walk."

The next day, I went to the hospital in the
afternoon and guess what? Mrs. Knolls was sitting
beside her bed in a wheelchair!

"What took you so long to get here?" She
asked me.

I told her I was sorry, but I was there now and we could go for our walk. They sent her back to the nursing home and she was with us for a few more months.

One day, as I sat next to her and saw the pain that she was in, I asked, "Mrs. Knolls, why don't you just go and be with Jesus?"

She very sternly said, "How can you say that? Who would pray for all the people that I pray for, if I went to be with Jesus?"

I had no answer so I apologized for my lack of faith.

A New Experience

Mark 6:13
...They anointed with oil many who were sick, and
healed them.

Miss Bessie was an elderly neighbor that got sick and was sent to the hospital. The Holy Spirit prompted me to go visit her. Before I left, He asked me to take a bottle of oil with me.

When I got to the hospital The Spirit said, *"Anoint her with oil and pray for her to be healed."*

My response was, "Only if I am in the room by ourselves."

When I walked up to the waiting room, her family was sitting together and told me that she was in a room down the hall. There was no one else in her room.

So I took out the oil, anointed her and prayed for her healing. At that point, I had never done anointing or praying for healing before.

The next day, to the family's joy, Miss Bessie came home! Praise God, He listened to my prayer!

The Healing Touch

I Corinthians 3:3
... For where there are envy, strife, and divisions among you, are you not carnal behaving like mere men?

While we were living in Tennessee and attending a Presbyterian church I had a Sunday school class of teenagers and we decided it would be fun to do a play of the trial of Christ for Easter. We had costumes and the kids wrote the script. It was a powerful play for them.

One day at dress rehearsal, the boys were making fun of the young man who was portraying King Herod because he was in a robe. They started scuffling. They pushed the young man and made him fall against the wooden pew. Immediately his face began to swell and his eye was swollen shut.

I walked over to him and said, "Oh, forgive them." And I touched his eye and it was healed. I stood amazed!

Thank you Father, for your power to heal.

My Back is Healed

Psalms 107:1-2
*Oh, give thanks to the Lord, for He is good! For
His mercy endures forever. Let the redeemed of the
Lord say so, whom He has redeemed from the hand
of the enemy*

There was a time in my life when I was
dealing with a back problem. It was to the point
that I could only crawl to get where I wanted to go.

I was crying out to God, "I can't live my life
like this. You've got to do something to heal my
back."

My husband said, "You're never going to
get well if you just lay in that bed all the time."

He proceeded to leave the room and told me
over his shoulder, "I am going in to town. I'll do the
weed eating when I get back."

After he left, I told the Lord, "Father, I am
going to claim my healing and I am going to get up
from this bed. I'm going outside and do the weed
eating! Is that a deal?"

To my surprise, when I stood up, I had no
pain. I walked outside, picked up the weed eater
and cut down the weeds.

My husband came driving up the driveway and saw me, he got out of the truck and yelled at me, "What are you doing?"

I told him the truth, "God has healed me. My back doesn't hurt any longer."

Boy, were we surprised!

Chapter 9

The Holy Spirit

This chapter is probably the most important because it teaches how the Holy Spirit is our helper. Christ promised that He was going to give us another Helper from the Father (John 14:16). I hope you will be inspired to try some of my methods for walking and listening to your Helper. I encourage you to ask the Father for the Holy Spirit as it says to do in Luke 11:13. The Holy Spirit teaches and gives us gifts to be used for a life worthy of our calling.

The Helper

John 14:16
*I will pray to the Father, and He will give you
another Helper, that He may abide with you
forever.*

I knew that Jesus had told his Disciples that
God would give us the Holy Spirit, but I did not
understand how He was going to be my helper. I
told God I was ready to start the transformation.

When I was reading the book of Galatians, I
read about the Fruit of the Spirit. These were
character traits of Jesus: love, joy, peace,
faithfulness, patience, kindness, goodness,
gentleness and self-control. I realized that if I was
going to be changed to be like Jesus it would be
important to have the Holy Spirit work these traits
into my character. How He planned to do this was
beyond my understanding, but I was positive if I
yielded to Him it would begin to happen.

I prayed, "Lord Jesus, Son of God fill me
with your Spirit."

As the Holy Spirit began changing me, I
noticed trials in my life. I remembered James 1:2-3,
*Count it all joy when you fall into various trials
knowing that the testing of your faith produces
patience.* Patience was one of the character traits.
Could it be that the Holy Spirit had begun His work
in me? Praise God.

I was intrigued with the Holy Spirit, so I did a study in the New Testament. I had always read my Bible but now I was growing more interested in learning to know more about my "new friend". I read in John 14:16, *I will pray to the Father, and He will give you another Helper, that He may abide with you forever.* This is what I needed, a Helper, so I began studying about the Holy Spirit.

In 1 Corinthians 3:16, the Word said, *Do you not know that you are the temple of God and that the Spirit of God dwells in you?* Then I read about the Fruit of the Spirit in Galatians 5:22, *Love, joy, peace, faith, patience, kindness, goodness, gentleness, and self-control.* I found out in Ephesians 4:30 we were not to grieve the Holy Spirit by letting our flesh control us rather than following the Spirit's guidance.

Because He is a gentleman He will not force His ways upon us. If we sin, we must go to the Father and confess our sins. Now I yielded my old nature to Him and let Him take control. This is how I began praying. When I was aware of my old nature rising up I would say, "I belong to the Lord Jesus Christ and I am not going to yield to my old nature."

Learning to Walk in the Spirit

Galatians 5:16
I say then: walk in the Spirit, and you shall not
fulfill the lust of the flesh.

At church I was helping a young girl who was struggling with a drug addiction. I asked her if she would be willing to go to a drug counselor and she agreed. I made an appointment for her. After she had spoken to the counselor and we were ready to leave, the counselor asked me to come into his office.

When I sat down he said, "I have a message for you from God. He wants me to tell you that soon you will begin to know the difference between your voice, the enemy's voice and the Holy Spirit's voice."

This was exciting and I couldn't wait to see if He was telling me the truth. Richard often left me a list of things he wanted me to do for that day. I decided to use this list as an experiment. I asked God to have the Holy Spirit remind me of the things I needed to do and to tell me the order in which He wanted me to complete them. If I didn't hear correctly it would not really be a problem.

So, I watched as the Holy Spirit began putting order to the things that had to be done. It was interesting to see that if I followed His plan my day went more smoothly.

I noticed that when I got home the Holy Spirit had neglected to direct me to pick up the back issues of the Mother Earth magazine from our friend. I quickly scolded the Holy Spirit and told Him these magazines were the most important items on the list to Richard. I was still scolding Him when the phone rang; it was the friend that had the back issues of the magazines that Richard had wanted me to pick up. She had called to apologize for not being home to give me the magazines.

After the phone call I immediately apologized to the Holy Spirit for not trusting Him. He knew our friend wasn't at home, so there was no need to stop at her house. It was nice knowing I had a helper and it proved to me that it was possible to allow Him to have charge of my day.

This was exciting to me. I realized I could trust the Holy Spirit. Now I would begin a new life of walking in the Spirit.

Why did I say No?

1 Corinthians 12:8
For to one is given the word of wisdom through the
Spirit, to another the word of knowledge through
the same Spirit…

I invited a friend to come to our house for dinner. As we sat talking, she said that she was moving to another state.

Out of my mouth came, "No, you must not move!"

She looked at me with a shocked look on her face. I understood that the Holy Spirit had just given me a word of knowledge. But to explain this to her would have been rather difficult.

The next day she called me and asked, "Why did you tell me that I shouldn't move?" I felt that what I had told her was God speaking to her through the Holy Spirit.

"You didn't know I was pregnant did you?" She asked.

"No, I didn't know" I replied.

Then I told her, "I believe I need to pray with you."

I realized that the reason that she was moving was because she was un-wed and ashamed of her pregnancy. She didn't want other people to know about it. She didn't want to have an abortion but didn't want her family to know either. I prayed for her to have God's guidance and wisdom. She said she would call me and we would talk later.

To my surprise, she called the next day and said that she had just had a miscarriage and needed me to take her to the hospital. I was surprised that this had happened. Was it the hand of God? I believe it was. I was reminded of the scripture, *God's ways are not our ways. We don't understand His will at times, but He works everything out for our good.*

She went on to live a normal life, got married and no one else ever knew.

Chapter 10

Helpful Hints

These Helpful Hints seemed to be stories that didn't fit in any of the other chapters, so I labeled them Hints. I hope they can help you in your relationship with God.

Devotions

II Timothy 4:7
I have fought the good fight, I have finished the
race, I have kept the faith.

There were things that happened in our life that I feel brought Richard to a better understanding of who God was. One of them was having devotions with the children once they had gotten old enough. But the very first time I started our devotions, Richard got up and went into the den to read his paper.

I prayed "This is not acceptable Father, please help me." So after the children went to bed, I sat down and spoke to Richard about his conduct.

I said, "Richard, this is very important to me, that my children understand the Bible and God's ways. When you get up and leave, you're saying this isn't important and I'm sure they think 'Why should it be important to us?' So I would appreciate it if you would not leave during our devotion time."

He said, "I understand, but you have to promise me that you won't ask me to answer any questions."

I agreed.

I began by reading a story from the Bible and then we would talk about it. When the children were older our devotions became a time of sharing the day's events and how God had worked in our lives. Then we would discuss what we needed to pray about. God used our devotion time to bring us closer to Him and we were all taught God's word. The habit of devotions has developed a family time with us and we continue to this day.

God Created Love for Jen

John 13:35
"By this all will know that you are My disciples, if
you have love for one another."

There was a new lady at church named Jen.
Instead of reaching out to her in friendship like we
should have, we would talk about her and all of the
things she did that irritated us.

One day while praying, the Holy Spirit
convicted me of my unloving attitude towards this
lady. One of the jobs of the Holy Spirit is to
convict us of our sins and shows us how to walk in
God's will. Praise God, He was helping me to see
my sin! I asked God to forgive me and to create
love in my heart for her.

It was interesting how I found myself being
placed in meetings, classes and the choir with Jen.
We ended up being together every Wednesday night
at practice. One day, I noticed that I was developing
a friendship with Jen. Praise the Lord! He had
created love in my heart for her. In my eyes it was
a miracle!

If you want to have the same love for a
person, just ask the Holy Spirit to create this love in
your heart for them. I thanked God that He had
shown me His way of love.

How Can He Use Me?

John 14:26
But the Helper, the Holy Spirit, whom the Father
will send in My name, He will teach you all things,
and bring to your remembrance all things that I
said to you.

Sally was a friend of my daughter, and she
became my friend too. One day, she told me how
hard it was for her to read the bible.

"Ask the Holy Spirit to help you," I told
her. "He is the one who wrote it and I am sure He
will help." She thanked me and we ended the
conversation.

A few days later she called and said, "I have
a surprise for you. Will you come out to my house
for lunch tomorrow?"

When I got to her house I said, "What's the
surprise?"

"I accepted Jesus as my Savior!" She told
me.

"I thought He already was your Savior" I
replied.

"I didn't think you knew I wasn't a
believer." She said.

"When you told me to ask the Holy Spirit to help me, I said to God 'I think my friend has this backwards. I think I need Jesus first,' so I prayed and asked him into my heart."

It's amazing how God can use me even when I'm confused about a person.

I Have Eternal Life

Romans 6:23
For the wages of sin is death, but the gift of God is
eternal life in Christ Jesus our Lord.

While I was in Denver at the Asthma Clinic
with my son, the Holy Spirit woke me early one
morning and told me *that I would meet Nancy and*
tell her about eternal life. Since the Holy Spirit had
told me that I would meet Epi just the day before I
felt confident He would arrange for me to meet
Nancy today.

When I got to the clinic they asked me if I
would mind staying with a young girl who was not
able to go on the field that had been planned for the
day. I agreed and thought it would be fun.

When they brought the young girl in and
introduced her, to my surprise, her name was
Nancy. She was so young!

I told God, "You need to have her ask me
about eternal life. She seems too young to
understand this concept."

All day long we played games and did fun
things but we never talked about eternal life. When
the young people came back from the field trip,
someone turned on the TV and it was the Merv
Griffin show. He was interviewing George Burns

and asking him about how long he planned to live. Mr. Burns didn't have an answer.

Then Nancy asked me, "Do you know when you are going to die?"

"I have eternal life because I believe in the Lord Jesus Christ." I answered

.

"Really?" She asked.

Then I was able to share with her the plan of salvation.

A Time to Pray

James 1:5
If any of you lacks wisdom, let him ask of God, who gives to all liberally and without reproach, and it will be given to him.

How many times have you stood in line at the bank or the grocery store and become frustrated?

Well this seemed to be happening to me all the time so I asked God, "Can you please help me?"

My way of dealing with it had always been to hop into the shortest line and get out of there quickly. God showed me that it was a perfect time to pray. So I would begin praying and found pleasure in waiting in lines.

Try it, sometimes it works!

God's Help

1 Peter 4:8
And above all things have fervent love for one
another, for "love will cover a multitude of sins."

I asked God to give me things I could do to reach out in acts of love toward my husband. Greeting him with the children at the door each evening was one thing I began doing. I gave up Wednesday night church and we had a family night of fun.

When I did this, it surprised Richard and he asked me, "Have they stopped having church on Wednesday night?"

I explained that the Holy Spirit had suggested this plan. I sometimes even thought that the going to church on Wednesday night—which is a good thing—needed to be replaced with doing something that my husband would rather do. This showed love and respect to him. We would play games or watch TV together. We watched a lot of football on the weekends and it gave Richard an opportunity to teach us about the game he loved. Even working together on the farm was more fun when done as a family.

All these things helped us grow and bond together. God's grace rebuked my selfishness and replaced it with time for my family. This behavior began to change my attitude and that affected my husband. I think this was God's way of teaching us the importance of family time together.

Living the Word

James 1:22
But be doers of the Word and not hearers only,
deceiving yourselves.

One morning as I talked with God I told Him how hard it was for me to memorize the Word.

The Holy Spirit told me, *"Many people can memorize the word, but few live it. I want you to live it."*

Each scripture I started to live had been a real struggle. I realized that God had very little control of my life. But when He brought a new scripture to walk in, I would yield and begin the road to change.

I knew His grace was sufficient for me. If I procrastinated I found the task was harder and it took longer for me to accomplish. It became an adventure working hand in hand with the God of the universe to change my ways and walk in His will.

Puppets Praise the Lord

Matthew 2:10
When they saw the star, they rejoiced with
exceedingly great joy.

One year I was asked to teach a Sunday school class of sixth graders. They had begun falling away from attending Sunday school. This was a real challenge and I prayed for God's help. He showed me how to use my Marionette puppets to bring a little spark of interest to the Sunday school program.

I went to each backslidden student's home and introduced them to my puppets and my plan for the class. I explained how I wanted the students to choose a Bible story they wanted to perform and they would write their own script. Then they would have to learn to perform using the puppets on the stage. I was surprise that many of the students came back to Sunday school class to have fun learning God's word and how to be puppeteers.

Our pastor asked if we could give a performance for the congregation and we agreed. We chose to do the Christmas story. When the time came for the Three Kings to enter the stage the boys used their puppets to make the kings leap and jump! I immediately asked God to not let anyone take offense at how the boys made the Kings act.

145

After the performance the pastor came up to me and said. "I will never read the Christmas story again without seeing the three Kings leaping and dancing with joy! Thanks for your student's interpretation of the Christmas story".

I thanked God and realized that he probably would like us to dance with joy at His son's birth.

Practice What You Preach

James 2:15-16
If a brother or sister is naked and destitute of daily
food, and one of you says to them, "Depart in
peace, be warmed and filled," but you do not give
themthe things which are neededfor the body, what
does it profit?

The church I attended would send members
of our congregation to march in front of the
abortion clinic. My son and his friend asked me if I
would go with them and I said no. They were
shocked and asked me why I wouldn't go? I said I
did not believe that it was the method that God
would choose.

I told them that if everyone who marched
against abortion would take one of the girls who
were pregnant into their home and take care of them
for the duration of the pregnancy and show them
love, there wouldn't be as many abortions. They
understood what I was saying was the truth so they
didn't go either. My son asked me to tell the church
what I had told him, so I asked permission to share
my idea. The congregation said it was a good plan
for me and that it would probably work, but they
didn't want to commit to it.

It was interesting how God gave me the
opportunity to back up what I had said. Would I
practice what I had preached? At the time I was
working on a help line, praying for people who

called to ask for help. One particular day after I had told the church how I felt, a young girl called the help line and asked for prayer. Her parents wanted her to get an abortion and her boyfriend agreed, giving no support or help.

The Holy Spirit prompted me to invite her into my home. She was amazed that I could offer such a thing.

She took my number and said, "After I have the baby I will call you." So I waited for her call.

By the time we met and got together I had a place for her in our old farmhouse. She lived there until she was able to get on her feet. We are still friends to this day.

Richard Asks for Devotions

Romans 10:14
How then shall they call on Him in whom they have
not believed? And how shall they believe in Him of
whom they have not heard? And how shall they
hear without a preacher?

Our children went off to college, and
Richard and I were left with an empty nest. When
the children were at home, we would have
devotions each day. But after they were gone, I just
neglected to have devotions.

One day, Richard said to me, "Are you
going to do your thing?"

"My thing?" I asked. "What is my thing?"

"You know, where you read in the Bible;
you ask questions and talk about what it says," he
replied.

"Oh, you want to have devotions!" I
exclaimed. "Sure! That's wonderful."

Sometimes when we would be praying, he
would tell me how I forgot to mention someone or
something he thought was important in my prayer.

I would say to him, "You ask about thus and
so. I didn't think about it, so it must be your
prayer."

He was just silent and never spoke an
audible prayer, but I'm sure that he prayed silently.

God's Will

Romans 12:2
And do not be conformed to this world, but be
transformed by the renewing of your mind, that you
may prove what is that good and acceptable and
perfect will of God.

Self-examination of my heart for any selfish motives was a must. I wanted to come to the point where I was certain my only desire was to know and do God's will.

"How can I learn this Father?" I asked.

"By reading and studying My word" He answered.

These are some of the scriptures I found that helped me know God's will.

- *Be obedient. (Titus 3:1)*
- *Be yielded. (2 Chronicles 30:8)*
- *Desire God's will. (Matthews 5:16-18)*
- *Love thy neighbor as thy self. (John 15:12)*
- *Love the Lord with all thy heart and with all thy soul and with all your mind. (Deuteronomy 6:5)*
- *Live in fear of God. (Proverbs 9:10)*
- *Glorify God in every phase of our life. (1 Chronicles 6:20)*
- *Help carry one another's burdens. (Galatians 6:2)*

- *Be examples to others in all things. (1 Timothy 4:12)*
- *Present your bodies a living sacrifice Holy acceptable unto God which is our reasonable service. (Romans 12:1)*
- *Love one another as I have loved you. (Romans 13:8)*

This is quite a list of scriptures and now I had my work cut out for me. As I read the Word, the Holy Spirit drew me to scriptures that pointed out the things that I needed to work on such as lying. Lying was not a trait I was proud of and I was in agreement that it should go.

Anger also consumed me along with bitterness and others too numerous to mention. I wept many tears and begged for God to purify me.

God has a way of bringing circumstances into our lives that give us a chance to choose His ways or our old nature's ways. I want to give you an example of how God helped me to overcome my anger: One particular evening I walked into the kitchen and my husband pointed to a piece of paper laying on the floor.

He told me, "Don't just walk over that piece of paper, pick it up."

I became angry. My old nature wanted to lash out but instead I cried out to God: "If you don't do something I am going to do and say something you won't like."

Immediately I felt God's peace flowing in me and over me and I knew victory was mine. I very calmly walked over and picked up the piece of paper. This incident showed me that God's power was there for me if I would only cry out for God's help. *James 4:7* was true, *"submit yourself unto God resist the devil and He will flee from you."*

Chapter 11

Richard's Death

After Richard's death God seemed to take over and show me His hand of provision upon me. I will always remember how He took charge and showed me the way I could trust Him for my every need...

Isaiah 41:10
Fear not, for I am with you; be not dismayed, for I
am your God. I will strengthen you, Yes, I will help
you, I will uphold you with My righteous right hand.

After my husband, Richard was retired, we
planned to do a lot of traveling. Our camper was
perfect and very comfortable for the two of us. We
had invited my sister and her husband to go with us
to California to visit my brother. They planned to
come down from Indiana to our home in Tennessee
a few days before the trip.

Before we left, Richard and I began praying
for our trip. Our prayer was for God to go before us
and prepare the way. We thought God was
preparing my brother's heart to receive Jesus, but
little did we suspect how different our trip was
going to be.

As the May departure date drew closer, I
decided to ask God what book He would choose for
my sister and I to read for our devotions on the trip.
One came to my mind and I quickly ran upstairs to
find it. It was the Daughters of Eve, by Lottie B.
Hobbs.

When we started on our trip I showed my
sister the book I had brought. We decided to begin
that very morning. We rode in the back of our
camper while the men took turns driving. We
headed for our daughter's home in Colorado
because she and her friend were going with us to

155

Moab, Utah. Our first stop was Grand Junction,
Colorado where we found a motel room for the
girls.

The next morning was Richard's 64th
birthday so we decided to spend the day
sightseeing. Before we started, our young friend
went for a walk and found a rose bush in a vacant
lot beside the sidewalk. She picked a small bouquet
for the birthday boy.

That morning we traveled to Moab, Utah.
We were very impressed with the beauty of the red
rock formations. We stopped at a place called
Dewy Bridge. We all walked to the bridge. The day
was sunny and not a cloud in the sky. Richard and I
took off for the camper walking hand in hand. Then
suddenly he dropped my hand and began running.
Why he did this is a mystery.

"What's the matter?" I called to him.

Suddenly out of nowhere, a bolt of lightning
and a deafening clap of thunder came from the sky.
I screamed and closed my eyes. When I opened my
eyes again I saw Richard lying on the ground about
10 or 15 feet in front of me. I ran to him and began
to pray for God to raise him up and give him life. I
became hysterical so my brother-in-law took me to
a picnic table with the only shade tree in the area.

I knew I had to get control of myself. So I
decided to sing praises. I knew God inhibited the

praises of His people. I definitely needed God's presents, also singing scripture songs was very comforting to me.

The song I remember singing over and over was Isaiah 41:10: *Fear not for I am with thee. Be not dismayed for I am thy God. I will comfort thee, yea I will bless thee. I will uphold thee, with the right hand of thy righteousness.*

After a short while I heard God's words of comfort, *"Thank you my child for coming to me in your hour of need. Your loved one is with me in Paradise."* Now I knew Richard was dead but amazingly God had truly raised Richard up.

Soon the ambulance came and all five of us followed the police to the small town of Moab. No one had asked me any information; they just took Richard to a mortuary of their choosing. They took us into a room with a glass case filled with beautiful pottery urns. When the owner came to talk to me I told him my husband and I had decided years ago that we wanted to be cremated. He told me there were only two mortuaries in the town and only his had a crematorium. I praised God. I told him that since my daughter was a potter we did not need an expensive urn. He assured me that would be fine.

The police man came and told me my husband would have to be taken to Salt Lake City for an autopsy, which was the procedure in an accident of this type.

I looked him in the eye and said. "This will not be necessary."

He assured me that it was what had to be done. I asked him to go call the authorities and told him that I was sure that wouldn't be necessary in my husband's case.

The policeman went off to make the call and came back with a shocked look on his face.

"Lady, I don't know who you are," he said "but you are being taken care of today."

I told him my Heavenly Father was in charge of my life. I had asked Him to go before me to prepare every detail.

I was thankful that the owner of the mortuary gave us permission to park our camper in his parking lot until my daughter and her husband arrived from Denver.

We prepared to spend the night while the others left for the motel. As the night settled in we tried to get some rest. After laying there for a short time I prayed for God to help us sleep. God answered our prayer quickly and soon we were both sound asleep.

In the morning I felt like God was prompting me to read my devotion. I refused, but He was persistent so I got up and found the

Daughters of Eve devotional I had been reading with my sister. I opened it to a chapter about Naomi and Ruth who had both lost their husbands in—of all places—Moab! It taught me about being a widow. I began to cry. God had even prepared the devotion I would read. I was astonished.

I was startled by a knock on the door; it was the owner of the mortuary. He had brought us breakfast. Shortly after breakfast the owner knocked again and this time he had a small black box to give us; it was Richard's ashes. My daughter and I clung to each other crying and holding Richard's ashes between us.

In all the rush of the day, my brother had not been notified of Richard's death. Again, God had gone before us and had taken care of this detail. My brother's son was in Los Angeles driving on the freeway and listening to the radio. To his amazement the radio announcer said that Richard Miller of Fayetteville, Tennessee. had been struck by lightning in Moab, Utah. He drove home quickly and called the mortuary in Moab to verify what he had heard.

Later we all drove back to Denver where my son from Tennessee and adopted son met us and we began our caravan back home to Fayetteville.

Remember the bouquet of roses? Well they were still fresh as the day they were picked even in the hot camper all the way back to from Tennessee. What a miracle!

God reminded me of several very important things: Before we left on our trip, Richard had decided to sell our herd of cattle. He said he thought there was a risk of getting injured while dealing with them since we were getting older and we didn't need to take chances.

After we sold the herd, Richard decided to put in a heating and cooling system so we would not have to cut wood for heating our house. Then he decided to buy a new car. I agreed.

So when I got home, I was so thankful for God's provision! I didn't have to worry about the cows! I didn't have to worry about cutting wood! And... I even had a new car so I could be safe traveling on the road! God had gone before me and prepared the way again and again.

Chapter 12

How to Live as a Widow

After my husband's death I had to find out how to live as a widow. I wanted to learn how to set my own goals and then work to accomplish them. Through a bible study of the book of Ruth, I understood that I had choices. I could become bitter or I could yield my life to the Lord.

The First Steps to Becoming a Widow

Mathew 6:33
Seek ye first the kingdom of God and all of these
things will be added unto you.

After I made it home, I still had to learn to
live as a widow. Could I trust God to go before me
as He had so clearly on our trip?

One night about a week after getting home
from our trip, I was shopping. I looked at my watch
and it was 5pm. Richard always liked his dinner at
5:30, I must hurry home and fix dinner! Then I
suddenly realized I did not have anyone to fix
dinner for and I began to cry.

When I finally got control of myself I found
my car and drove to a friend's house, I knocked on
her door and asked if I could stay there for the
night. She graciously agreed. The next day I went
home and began asking God to help me adjust to
my new life without my husband.

I decided to join a bible study on the book of
Ruth. This was the book God had first used after
Richard's death. I realized that one study was not
enough for learning all I needed to learn. I needed
a lot of God's love to heal my broken heart.
I needed to fill my heart with something other than
the anger I felt towards God, so I joined four more
bible studies to fill my evenings.

Slowly I began to feel God's love but still the aching and loneliness would sometimes overwhelm me in the dark of the night. My tears were a way of bringing sleep, but sleep from crying is not a very restful sleep. I desperately needed a way to fill my life with purpose. I began thinking about setting goals. All my goals were Richard's goals and so now I had to have my own goals.

I decided to make a pond with a waterfall in the rock garden by the porch. I worked hard. The heat was horrible in June so I got up at 5:00 am while it was cool. I continued to work until it was too hot to work. My goal was to complete the pond by our wedding anniversary on July 28th, which gave me 6 weeks. When it was finished I was satisfied that I had reached my first goal. I had learned many things about myself and knew Richard would have been proud of my accomplishments. The waterfall gave me many relaxing hours as I sat in the porch swing listening to the peaceful sound of the water falling over the rocks.

God had used this project to show me I had the ability to create something beautiful. Now my next goal was to create a colorful flower garden, with a splash of color for every season. I was determined to make my yard a sanctuary in memory of Richard. The work was therapeutic. I found myself singing praise songs, something I had not done since I had returned home. I could even feel joy returning to my soul as I sat in the midst of nature.

Lonely Nights

Psalm 25:16-18
Turn Yourself to me, and have mercy on me, for I
am desolate and afflicted. The troubles of my heart
have enlarged; bring me out of my distresses! Look
on my affliction and my pain, and forgive all my
sins.

After my husband died I found it very hard to sleep on our bed in our Tennessee home. My friend was prepared by God to be free in the late night to talk on the phone. Her husband was on a business trip for a few months. This met my need for someone to talk to and cry out in my pain and loneliness. She listened and encouraged me by just letting me share my inner most anger and fears.

One night as I was talking about my anger with God my young friend very softly said, "Have you ever prayed the sinner's prayer?"

I was shocked that she felt I was a lost sinner in need of a prayer for Jesus! But as I thought quietly about all I had cried out to her during our conversations, I could see how she was led to believe I needed Jesus.

"You know that might be just what I need to do" I said.

So she led me in the sinner's prayer: *Dear Jesus, I believe you were born of the Virgin Mary*

and died on the cross for my sins and I have eternal
life. Thank you for your sacrifice.

After our prayer I thanked her for being my
friend. I felt peace and we said good-bye until the
next evening. I realized that I had not prayed for a
long time nor had I read my bible. Her question
made me realize that she thought I had lost my
salvation, but it wasn't that I'd lost my salvation,
but that I needed to re-dedicate my life to Christ and
allow Him to speak to me again. I decided it was
time to begin reading God's word again. I was also
able to pray with hope that I was forgiven for my
rebelliousness.

One of the most thrilling benefits of finding
new life in Christ is entering a new personal
relationship with God, that gives us a fullness of
spiritual vitality, and this new life is a gift that will
never die.

God Has a Plan

Psalm 56:3
Whenever I am afraid, I will trust in You.

From past experiences with God, I knew He would begin bringing circumstances for me to walk through in answer to my prayers. The first thing that happened was my widow friend, Soni came to visit me. As we sat talking I believe God was prompting me to ask her to come and live with me. We talked about the possibilities and she agreed to the idea. She was my companion for the next two years.

Having Soni live with me gave me someone to cook for, someone to talk to and someone to encourage me. She had walked this lonely path before. She shared with me some steps on grieving. I knew immediately the one I was experiencing and that was anger. I could feel my anger building up and I was becoming mad at God for taking Richard. I knew that if I did not begin to change I would soon become a bitter old woman who no one would want to be around and no one God could use.

It was helpful having a friend to share these difficult times with. Soni and I had been through many struggles together and this was just one more that we walked through together.

God Called Me into Service

Matthew 22:37
Jesus said to him, "You shall love the Lord your
God with all your heart, with all your soul, and with
all your mind."

One evening I went to an After Five Woman's meeting and the speaker was sharing about the need for volunteers in Jail Ministry. After the meeting I felt God tugging at my heart to talk to the speaker. She helped me begin my life of serving the young women at the local jail.

Oh, how I praise God for my young friend leading me in the sinner's prayer. God knew I needed help and He provided it. His help was there as long as I was willing to trust and obey.

The scripture, Matthew 22:37 came to life for me as I learned to love these young ladies that I was ministering to in jail.

A Hard Scripture for Me

I Thessalonians 5:16-18
Rejoice always, pray without ceasing, in everything
give thanks; for this is the will of God in Christ
Jesus for you.

One morning as I was reading the Bible I read I Thessalonians 5:16-18. This was a hard scripture for me to do. I told God I would never be able to give thanks for Richards's death. I might say the words but I would not mean it. I closed the bible and began to cry.

I don't remember how long it took me to pray that scripture with sincerity, but God was patient and helped me see His way was perfect.

New Home For The Bees and Me

1 John 5:14
Now this is the confidence that we have in Him, that
if we ask anything according to his will, He hears
us.

My young friend came to my aid again.
During one of our conversations we talked about
what to do with Richard's bees. I confessed that I
was afraid of those little creatures. She quickly said
she thought her husband would be interested and
sure enough he was. We then had to come up with
a plan to transport the bees from our farm to theirs. I
reminded her of my confession about being afraid
of bees—she assured me I would not be expected to
help.

Her husband came over in his truck and the
bees were moved with God's help to their new
home. I also had something else I wanted to have
moved. It was Richard's Lazy-boy chair, it made
me sad whenever I looked at it. So I offered it to
my friend's husband and he graciously took it off
my hands.

Everything that I didn't want to deal with of
Richard's had been taken care of. God knew my
needs as a widow and took care of everything.

A New Place To Sleep

Isaiah 43:18-19 (NIV)
Forget the former things; do not dwell on the past.
See, I am doing a new thing! Now it springs up; do
you not perceive it?...

One of the things I still found difficult was sleeping in our bed. I found it much easier to sleep on the couch. I asked God for His help and He began bringing the idea of making one side of our two-car garage into a bedroom. When Richard was alive we had talked about making a bedroom in the garage so we didn't have to climb the stairs when we got old. I began talking to my family about this idea and they thought it was something they could help with so the project began to take shape.

My sister and her husband came down from Indiana, my family from Colorado came down and my son also joined us. I ordered the materials for the room and we all came together for a room rising. With everyone's help we remodeled one side of the garage into a spacious bedroom and bath.

What a fun time with memories filling our hearts and minds forever.

This project, when finished, ended my sleepless nights. Praise God!

Moving to Colorado

2 Samuel 7:29
O Lord God, have spoken it, and with Your blessing let the house of Your servant be blessed forever.

I was still learning to be a widow on the farm in Tennessee, but everywhere I looked I was reminded of Richard. Our daughters both lived in Colorado and when Richard was alive I would teasingly say that if anything ever happened to him I was going to Colorado to live. Little did I realize at the time; God was planting that very desire in my heart.

So here I am in Colorado with my two daughters. My single daughter bought a home, which accommodates both of our needs. I thank God continually for taking care of me through the years.

It has been years since Richard's death and I am happy in Colorado. I have made new friends and I feel that I belong. Whatever God sees fit to bring into my life, I will rejoice and be glad. His plans are perfect and He will work all things together for good for those who love Him.

Home

On Wednesday June 8, 2016 Barbara was rushed to the hospital after a fall that resulted in a broken neck and puncture to her aorta artery. The doctors were able to revive her long enough for her to say goodbye to her family and friends. She was ready to be with her Heavenly Father so she did not want to be placed on Life Support if it came to that.

She spoke of rainbows and angels with her in the hospital room as she was ushered into heaven on Sunday, June 12, 2016. She praised and served her Savior up until her last breath.

A beautiful memorial service was held on June 23, 2016 at Rocky Mountain Christian Church in Niwot, Colorado. Friends and family members shared story after story of Barbara's love for God and others. She was an integral part of the Women's Ministry at RMCC and she will be greatly missed by so many.

This book was her last assignment and here are her final words to you:

"I pray that those who read this book will encounter the power of the Gospel. Romans 8:29: 'And

the Holy Spirit will transform the lives of those who are being conformed into the likeness of the Son.' This book is about how I learned to walk in the Spirit. As you read this book I pray that you will be inspired to have your own glorious adventure with God.

BELIEVE!"

Love,

Made in United States
Orlando, FL
13 February 2024

43676177R00104